D0501982

COLOUR
ENERGY®

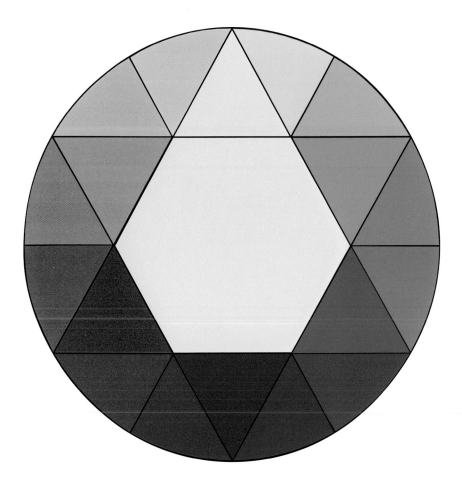

Copyright© 1996 Colour Energy

All rights reserved. No part of this publication may be reproduced or
transmitted in any form or by any means, electronic or mechanical, including
photocopy, without permission in writing from Colour Energy Corporation.
Reviewers may quote brief passages.

Colour Energy Corporation
P.O. Box 1743 Station A
Vancouver, B.C. Canada V6C 2P7

Printed in Canada
Graphic Design & Illustration: Agathe Christmar Storengen

Canadian Cataloguing in Publication Data

Naess, Inger, 1936 -
Colour Energy

1st English ed.
Translation of: Farve energi.
Includes Index.
ISBN 0-9680804-0-5

1. Color—Therapeutic use.
2. Color—Psychological aspects. I. Title

RM840.N3313 1996   615.8'31   C96-900921-6

INGER NAESS

COLOUR ENERGY

COLOUR ENERGY®

CONTENTS

PREFACE

I challenge you to read this book with a positive and open mind. Put away your skeptical and critical thoughts. These thoughts often belong to the negative side of the yellow and blue energies. If you block your world of experience with negative thoughts, criticism will never be objective. But if you open your senses and mind to new thoughts, you will give nourishment to your consciousness. When you have finished reading the book, your experience and wisdom will then judge the contents. And this criticism will be positive for both you and me. Write your thoughts down. These thoughts are valuable, because they can promote growth and new patterns of ideas. Always meet a new book with a virgin mind and a sense of curiosity.

This book is about colours and everything that colours can give us, including energy. Think about a rainbow. You can not touch or feel a rainbow. You do not know where it begins or where it ends. However, everybody knows that rainbows exist. I shall try to transmit some of the knowledge that is out there about colours. But most of what I will relay is how we at *Colour Energy* use the colours consciously to help us know ourselves better and all the people we would like to know better. We wish to teach the message that colours can change you and your world. Open the first page and enter a new room in your consciousness. Let the book relay its message to you. After that, you can be the critic. Enjoy!

Inger Naess

NOTE FROM THE AUTHOR

Before this book was planned to be published in English I never thought that a translator did anything more than translate words and sentences. But now I understand that translating is a highly specialized job. A translator is like an adventurer. S/he has to enter into every new book, and go into the writer's mind to translate not only the words but the rhythm and the hidden feelings that are behind every word. In my colour language, for example, we would say that the writer could be "orange" and that the translator could be "blue." This means that the blue translator would delete unnecessary words, as blue people are clever at getting to the point to make the content easier to read. On the other hand, the orange writer would like to embroider the facts to tell a story. So as you can see, in a translator's colourful world the translator has to have more than just the knowledge of how to translate.

I also would like to thank my violet energy drive. This energy lifts my thoughts towards a collective sky, and lets ideas and fantasies rain down on me. In the violet world everything is possible–even a book.

1

THE ART OF LIVING

We usually live partially in the past and partially in the future. Rarely do we manage to live completely in the present. Yet it is only by being in the "right now" that we can truly experience life. Everything in our body functions in the present—all our cells, all our organs. Our body's functioning is nourished and guided by information it receives directly from our soul, or spiritual consciousness. Only our thoughts are divorced from this direct communication with our soul. The more we exist in the present and allow the experiences of the present moment to dominate, the more we connect with our spiritual selves and are truly alive.

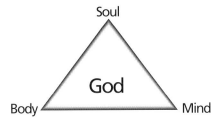

To live in harmony is to be in balance. We are in a state of highest consciousness when the Trinity of the soul, body, and mind—with God at the centre—is in balance. When our soul's emotional awareness, our mental awareness, and our physical body are all in harmony, we can experience life fully in the present moment. But we generally experience life in separate compartments: some people experience life through their intellect, others through feelings, still others through their body. Furthermore, there is enormous pressure on each of us to perform, produce, solve problems, and live in style. We think that to live wholly and completely is a kind of luxury that we don't have time for. We make excuses for our failure to live in the present moment: "It's hard enough trying to survive." "So much is expected of me, I have to plan ahead." "I don't have time to be myself." There are too many obligations, too many "I have to's" and "I must's."

But wait a second. I think there is a misunderstanding. Nobody is asking you to be more than who you already are with all of your problems, demands, and obligations. There is no need to change your life, or put time aside to be in the present moment. Words like "to live fully" and "to be yourself" describe a state of consciousness. We all have jobs and obligations; our days are too short and our nights too busy. But it is as simple as this: no matter what you do or who you are, you are a whole person. To be in the present simply means focusing your attention and concentration on what you are doing now. If you let your thoughts take over and wander from what you are doing, confusion and lack of energy will result. Furthermore, you cannot do two or three things simultaneously and do all of them one hundred percent. Therefore, let the activity or work you doing at the moment get all the attention and concentration it deserves. Thinking of things other than what you are presently doing often can cause mistakes to happen at work. What you do deserves your attention, but that is not the only thing—what you do deserves good and positive thoughts as well.

Thoughts are like streams of energy surrounding the things you do. For example, when you eat, you automatically conclude that the food is prepared with intention and kindness.

But consider this scenario:

A woman works in a cannery where they can sardines. Her husband is out of work and has begun to drink heavily. He becomes depressed and acts violently towards his wife. Every day begins with a fight with her husband, and she arrives at the cannery distressed and angry. With every sardine she packs, she curses her husband as the cause of all her problems. Each sardine can receives this flow of negativity. This continues, can by can, until the woman has emptied her aggression.

Consequently, her aggression gets passed onto the cans of sardines. Maybe for lunch you will be the one to open a can of "aggressive sardines." You then end up eating cursed sardines. You might be reading the daily newspaper while you are eating. Newspapers are full of negative news. This mix of negativity will influence you. Thoughts can produce strong vibrations. For example, negative and positive thoughts can change the smell in a room. They can change your aura, even your cell structure, and can certainly influence how you think and feel. Enjoy your meal!

Some people say living is an art. A few people even become masters at this art of living. The art lies in consciously balancing body and soul within the present moment, and in harmonizing the will and the willfulness of emotion.

This "art of living" is full of journeys. Yet it's not the destination that is the important thing. "The path is the goal!" and "the seeker feels at home on the path," are sayings that we know very well. It is not your goals in life that are important but how you deal with your daily problems. I prefer to say *assignments* instead of problems, because that is actually what they are. What you see as problems are assignments in disguise–exactly like math problems which are made more difficult by framing them in a story. It is so easy to just focus on the goal and believe that is what you are headed for. There is a catch to the goal, however. It is on the way towards the goal that you will find the assignments. It does not matter whether the assignments are big or small; the important thing is how you solve them to reach your goal. You have probably heard famous people talk about achieving their goals and how they starved and worked hard to reach them; once at their goal, they said that it was on the way to achieving their goal that they were the happiest.

Happiness is right now. And it is only when you are totally aware that you really know what happiness is. When you live a conscious life, you realize that you only have a given time on earth, and that you want to get the most out of that time. If you believe in reincarnation, you believe that all experience and all growth go to the soul as nourishment and are reserved for future incarnations. You can look to yourself in the same way and benefit from previously stored experiences. Most people have probably had the feeling of "this is right," or "I know that." This is called intuitive knowledge. It is knowledge that your soul already possesses. Life is exciting when you know that each human being has his or her own assignments to solve.

It is not only aware thought that can reside in the present moment. The body also knows how to live in the right now, but it needs understanding and love. How long has it been since you last gave yourself a pat on the back? How long has it been since you stroked your hands and thanked them for all the information they give you? Fingertips are sensory devices with the finest detectors. They give us thousands and thousands of pieces of information about textures, softness, heat, cold, etc. These sensations can evoke happiness, displeasure, fear, and malaise–it all depends on how we perceive and store the pieces of information we receive. We need to get in touch with our body and learn how our body uses sensations and the senses to communicate. A healthy body that has its needs taken care of and is comfortable and loved has no pain or sore spots.

Maybe there is an art to living after all. The difficulty is in trying to know yourself. You need to become so interested in yourself and your incredible machinery that you dedicate your whole life to learning how to live in harmony with yourself.

THE ART OF DYING

Our days are numbered, but who or what counts the days? How does the body know that it is going to die?

You have to know yourself–your good and bad sides–and be able to use your indigo intuitive energy if you want to know how long you have got. Many people have had an invitation to enter the other side and have been prepared. Many other people, though, have died without any forewarning or preparation. You cannot avoid death, and you cannot deny the fact that one day you will die. We all have to die. No doubt about it. Why don't we prepare ourselves better, increase our knowledge, and be a little more happy about the fact that one day we will die? We see death as the absolute end of life. But it is only an end to our physical life–an end to the physical human being we chose to live life through on this earth.

Reincarnation teaches us that our soul chose to be born as a human being in order to learn. In given family situations, with given hereditary genes, and given backgrounds there will be opportunities to learn assigned lessons. Do you get along with your parents? Do you have the most impossible siblings or in-laws on earth? Do not despair–they are present in your life so that you can learn lessons. You have to learn how to recognize yourself in them. Remember, the more you understand other people and human relationship difficulties, the easier it will be for you to fully understand yourself.

The Art Of Dying

"Life is like a school and death is like an exam." Most of us dread an exam. Is it because you were not sufficiently prepared? Did you not study or did you not understand the assignment? Were you unenthusiastic about studying? This is what life is like as well. Maybe you chose to follow the wrong route. Nevertheless, the exam will happen, perhaps before you have had time to clarify and do all the things that you never had time to do. Life and death are closely connected. They are two in one. That is why it is so important to know what life is and to understand that life happens in the right now. To live is present tense. Death is welcome if you have lived in the present and have wrapped up loose ends every day. Your time is preordained. Everyone has time limits printed in every cell and in every line on the palm of their hand. But who really wants to know when it is their time to go? You perhaps believe that you can overcome death if you have survived a terminal illness or a near-fatal accident with the help of skillful doctors, but no—you do not fool death. Your time on earth is set.

I do not understand why there is so little interest in the aging and dying process. Why are we not interested in what happens when we die? How do I die? What happens to my body when I die? What can I do to help? How can I die and take an active part in it? Do you not like to talk about death? Well, did you know that many other great cultures have incorporated the art of living and dying in their life philosophy.

How to prepare for death is part of the Tibetan teachings about life, and is explained in the *Tibetan Book of the Dead*. Let me introduce you to a part of *The Tibetan Book of Living and Dying*, written by Sogyal Rinpoche. It's about what happens to your body when you die.

It has been said that when you are born you are actually dying, and when you die you are actually being born. You have already forgotten who you were. If you have been present when a person has died, you will have seen the opal, yellow-coloured face and hands of the dying person. This is a manifestation of the cloud of lower energies, which held the physical body together and is now in the process of leaving the body. The upper chakras or energy centres also begin to open. The death process begins when the energies of your chakras start to separate. The lower red and orange energies separate from the upper indigo, blue, and violet energies.

During a three-hour period, starting with the first hour after death, you feel that all the different energy centres are being washed by a golden beam which leaves the head through the crown chakra. The crown chakra has now developed a yellowish white colour. People who have had near death experiences feel that they have lived their whole life over. And that is what happens. All the blockages in the physical body are dissolved and washed clean. The body is free. Death has purified the body and the soul goes on its way to a new dimension. Or more simply, the soul is on its way home. If you are lucky enough to know that you are about to die, or if the family around the bed senses that death is near, you can prepare for death. You can prepare for death by being in the right position. Lie on your right-hand side with your right hand under your chin to enable you to close the right nostril. This is called the Buddha position. The left hand is lying loosely on the left side. On the right side of the body, there are certain channels that encourage the "karmic wind." When you lie on the right side closing the right nostril, you help to block these channels, so that it is easier for you to recognize the light when death is near. Moreover, if your channels are blocked, your consciousness can leave the body through the crown chakra more easily. Our senses are the first to disappear when we die. If there are people around your bed when you die, you will hear their voices, but you will not be able to hear the words. This means that the hearing process has stopped functioning. It will not be long before your sight starts to weaken. You will be able to see the outlines of a person, but not the details. This means that the sight process has stopped functioning. The same happens to the senses of smell, taste, and touch. When the senses do not function anymore, you enter the next phase of death.

You Lose Contact With Your Physical Body

First our body loses its strength and all our energy weakens. We can no longer stand or hold on to things. We cannot even hold up our heads. We get a feeling of sinking into the ground or being pinned by an enormous force, as if a mountain is squashing us. We feel heavy and uncomfortable in all positions. We might ask to be lifted a bit and get our pillow fluffed. Our skin begins to lose its colour. Our cheeks fall in and dark spots appear on our teeth. It gets harder and harder to open our eyes. We become weak. Our thoughts diffuse and in the end we sink into a world of fog. A "secret sign" that tells you what phase you are in appears in your consciousness. The secret sign for this phase is a vision of a shimmering mirage.

You Lose Contact With Feelings

This is the sign that the earthly element has been abandoned and that we are on our way into the water element. We start to lose control of our bodily fluids. Our noses start to run, fluid may flow from our eyes, and water leaves the urinary system. We can no longer move our tongue, our eyes feel dry, our lips are bloodless, and our mouth and throat feel dry. Our nostrils dilate. We tremble as the smell of death hangs over us. As our capacity to feel disappears, we alternate between sensations of pain and well-being, heat and cold. Our mind becomes foggy, frustrated, irritable, and nervous. Some have said that it feels as if you are drowning in the ocean or being swept away by a big wave that pulls you down. The secret sign is a vision of a haze of heat and clouds of smoke. The fire element takes over when the water element disappears.

You Lose Contact With Heat

Our mouths and noses dry up completely. All heat leaves the body, usually from the feet towards the heart. Some heat may leave through the crown chakra. The breath is cold as it comes out of both the mouth and the nose. We can no longer drink or eat. Our consciousness goes from clarity to confusion. We can no longer remember names of family and friends or even who they are. It becomes more and more difficult to keep in contact with our surroundings as both sight and sound are confused. It might feel as if you are surrounded by flames, as if you are in the middle of a roaring fire, or as if the entire earth is burning up in flames. The secret sign is a shimmer of red sparks over an open fire, just like fireflies.

You Lose Contact With Air

It becomes harder and harder to breathe. All the air seems to disappear right through the throat. We start to huff and puff. Our breathing becomes short and gasping, and our exhalation longer. Our eyes roll backwards and we are totally immobile. Our thoughts become more and more confused by the outer world as our intellect dissolves. Everything becomes confusing. Our last sense of our physical surroundings is that they are slipping away. We have hallucinations and visions. If we have experienced many negative things in our lives we may see frightening forms. All the terrible incidents in our lives are replayed and we feel that we shall scream in fear. If we have lived a life of happiness and kindness, we may experience a moment of good memories and of meeting good friends. For those who have lived a good and rich life there is peace in death, not fear. The dying person feels as if a strong wind has swept the whole world, including her/himself, into a whirlpool. This wind is part of the whole universe. The air element is dissolving into the consciousness. The secret sign is a vision of a flaming lamp with a red glow.

Our inhalations become weaker and weaker, and our exhalations longer. At this point the blood gathers in the "life channel," going to the centre of the heart. Three drops of blood collect, one after the other. They constitute three long and final exhalations, and after that we breathe no longer. Only a low heat remains in the heart. All other vital signs are gone. It is at this point a doctor would pronounce you clinically dead. This is the most common way to die. All living creatures, from insects and up, die like this. The same would happen much faster if you died in a fatal accident.

I think this explanation is great. I would like to know what will happen when I die. I wish there was someone like a "death guide," who could teach us about the road of death that we all have to walk, and who could also teach us to look forward to death with a little happiness and excitement.

REINCARNATION

This is the simplest explanation for reincarnation:

Everybody has a soul.

The soul survives the death of the physical body.

The soul is part of other dimensions.

The soul chooses to be reincarnated.

The soul chooses what it wants to learn in the next life.

The soul is reincarnated in a new physical human being to continue to develop positive and negative physical and spiritual life values.

This cycle repeats itself until the soul has positively developed all physical and spiritual life values, which then get transformed into more conscious energy. At this point the soul stops reincarnating into a body, and now serves the human race at a pure spiritual level.

Reincarnation is acknowledged in most parts of the world and in most religions. Christianity has not acknowledged reincarnation although the Bible contains many writings about the issue. Reincarnation is just as unprovable as heaven and hell. Faith has to build on instinct and on the inner feeling of what is right. I feel that my life is richer and truer by believing in reincarnation. It makes it more fun to work on myself. It is like a relay race where I leave some of my stride to the next runner. Last but not least, I feel immortal.

ABOUT ENERGY

Nobody knows what keeps a person alive. We know that we consist of many complex proteins, organs, and nerves, which work as a whole and perfect machine. But what is the spark? What makes us tick, and why? Our bodies consist of molecules, one on top of each other, and organs connected to other organs in an incredible chain of perfection. Do you think that is all there is to life? Do you think that man is limited to existence only? No, there is so much more.

> We are connected to all living creatures.
> Moreover, we are connected to the universe.
> We are not alone.

It is no accident that we were born. Do you think that evolution stops with human beings, here and now? Are human beings the most perfect product of evolution? And, if we believe in the evolution theory, what does it take to make human beings better? And what are we going to become? The answers lie in the future, but the most important thing is that we realize that we are fantastic biochemical factories with unlimited possibilities, both mental and physical.

We have access to pure energy. Light is life. Light is our source of energy. The sun sends a constant stream of energy to our earth. Everything reaches for this energy. Even if it is raining, the sun is still shining above the clouds and sending its energy through every raindrop. In that way the rain is both water and intense solar energy. If you look into a raindrop in the right way you will see a rainbow reflection.

Everything that lives in and on the earth exists because of solar energy. We live because the earth provides us with crops of food. The sun bombards the earth with light at a speed of 300,000 kilometres per second. This light vibrates with colour energies, which we absorb through our eyes and skin. We cannot live without light energy. Yet we take light for granted, as we take the necessary life energy for granted. It is not until illness eats up our energy reserves, and we feel that our energy is disappearing, our body weakened and our mental will inadequate to make the body function with vitality, that we realize how essential life's energy sources are. It is like a dam without water when the body is drained of energy.

About Energy

Imagine that you are your own power plant. The sun's energy and everything the sun touches with its rays are always readily available. That means we have access to energy through everything that lives.

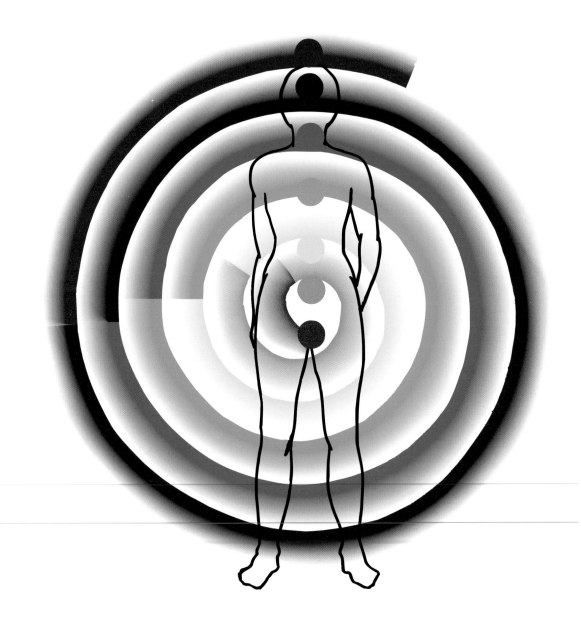

Now imagine that you have seven main power stations where you can store energy. You must ensure that there is clear passage between the different stations, as the power stations are linked to each other. Experts say that a blockage of a power station happens when a physical or psychic event is repeated over and over again, or endured for extended periods of time. Depending on where your weak spots are and how big the blockage is, illness can result. Another name experts use for the energy power stations is "chakra." These seven stations have different transformer systems. First, we have a low running base station, the red energy centre or chakra. This red base station is situated in the lower back. The energy from the red base station moves to other stations like this:

The stations are like interlocking wheels which allow the energies to go up and down according to which special energy you need. At the top or crown power station is the fast and highly gifted violet energy; at the bottom is the vigorous, happy red energy.

These are our power stations; these are our energy sources. Think how powerful and resourceful our bodies are. Our physical body is like a home for our free soul and our free thought. Our free soul and free thought are totally independent of time and place, but they have to work with a physical, material body. This body is like a power plant with access to energy. Imagine the possibilities if free soul and thought used this power plant in the human body. Imagine if the free soul and thought used ideas, a kind heart, and careful planning to take energy from this power plant. Bees fly from flower to flower to gather nectar; in the same way, we get energy from the different stations. Man has been made in the image of God, and s/he has given us all the power between heaven and earth.

Feeling Colours–The Blind Who Could See

When we talk about colours, we usually talk about seeing colours. What about people who are blind? Can they feel colours? We made a series of radio programs about COLOUR ENERGY®, *and one of them featured Norwegian artist*

About Energy

Magna Jensen. Though Magna is completely blind, she paints the most beautiful colour pictures. As part of an experiment, we had Magna feel blankets in red, blue, and green and tell us the right colour. "Red" said Magna, as she indeed picked up the red blanket. "I recognize the good warm feeling." She then picked up the blue blanket. "I recognize blue by the tingling cold feeling." Magna said that it's easiest for her to recognize the pure primary colours, and so she had a small problem with the colour green. Green is a neutral colour and a mix of yellow and blue. Confusion can occur when a cold and a warm colour are mixed. "To know colours is like winning an Olympic medal," said Magna. "You need to work long and hard to get results and I work at it every day." Magna developed her ability to feel colours by touching plants. She learned the difference between the green leaves and the red flowers. Moreover, Magna told us that her blindness has given her a richer life in many ways. "I have become much more sensitive in a positive way. It is so much easier to discover your inner universe when you no longer see the outside world."

Lately, I have become very involved in the world of the blind. I used to think that being blind was the worst disability one could possibly have, but now I have changed my mind.

Recently I read the book, "And There was Light", by the French writer Jacques Lusseyran, who became blind when he was eight years old. His life became something of a fairy tale thanks to his good nature and his positive indigo energy. Nothing stopped him from living a normal life. He was only seventeen years old when he became involved with the French resistance movement. Earlier, he had learned Braille and put himself through school. He passed every exam with honours. He was even accepted at university. He was a typical yellow/blue intellectual, but his indigo energy helped him out the most. He had no problem using indigo energy whenever he needed it. He developed his intuition, understanding, and inner voice, which directed and protected him in the last part of the war.

Jacques Lusseyran was one of the principal writers of the illegal newspaper "Defense de la France", (later "France Soiree"), which reached all of France through an enormous distribution net. During W.W.II Jacques helped manage this newspaper. In the end he was captured and was sent to the Buchenwald concentration camp. Over 380,000 people died in this camp, mostly Russians, Yugoslavs, Belgians, Danes, and Poles. Only 20 out of 2,000 French prisoners survived, and Jacques was one of them. Jacques said himself that the "light" helped him. From the moment he became blind, he had to use his other senses, and he learned to trust these senses. He became in tune with his body. He sensed and understood the outer and inner mechanism of his body. He discovered his fingers, his sense of touch. Before becoming blind, his fingers did not sense anything. But now they were "alive" and told many things. He felt the life pulse of all things and this gave him answers. Through his sense of touch, everything existed and had its own life.

It was the same with his sense of smell. He started to realize how animals felt when they sniffed. For him smell became both physical and emotional. He could smell fear, anxiety, and cowardice. His sense of hearing also became more finely tuned. He could accurately judge the height of buildings. He developed a sympathy with nature. Jacques saw all the colours of the rainbow through his inner light. To him colours were so beautiful that he could barely describe them. Colours became his friends. During the last years in Buchenwald, many remaining survivors became sick. Jacques was able to give comfort to them, drawing strength from an inner source of light. He learned a lot in the camp, especially from the Russians—not the intellectuals but the casual labourers, the poor. The poor, that no one noticed in the normal society, were the ones who survived. They did not give up or lose hope. They did not complain but helped each other. They cared about each other and did not think only about themselves. They developed inner peace and happiness by helping each other and by not being afraid. In this setting you would see a good citizen steal bread from his brothers and a simple thief share bread with a dying person. Jacques learned important lessons: he learned that fear kills, that happiness creates life, and that you must live in the here and now.

Living in the present moment saved Jacques, because he did not worry about tomorrow. He made the best of every day. Just knowing that he still existed, despite all the suffering, gave him an inner light and happiness. He spread this inner light to others.

I would like to mention another famous Norwegian blind person, Erling Stordal. On his seventieth birthday he was asked in a newspaper interview what he would wish for if he had three wishes. Surprisingly, being able to see was not among his three wishes.

What do these three blind people have that we do not have? I think that they have learned to trust their inner self, to listen to a different sense other than sight. We, with our sight, have forgotten that we have an inner sensory device that can help us. It is similar to an animal's sense of awareness in the dark. We have forgotten how to develop and use this sense. In a way we have become dependent on sight. The same thing has happened with calculators and computers. We have let them take over our mental calculations and our control of manual work. Progress can be great. I use a computer, but I think that it is important to learn how to be independent of mechanical help. Like the blind, we should not let sight and visual impressions become the only determining factor in judging other people. Maybe we need to become open to other signals.

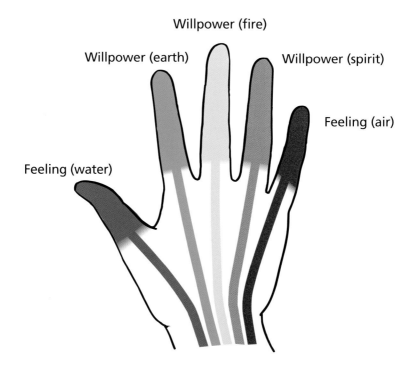

WHAT ARE WE?

Many people have pondered this question. Scientists have dissected the human body in every possible way to find out what makes us tick, and what have they found out? Physicists and mathematicians are advanced in their theories about the universe. But what are we?

The DNA molecule is the most complex molecule ever found in nature. The double chain of DNA molecules is the electrochemical messenger of life. The DNA molecule plays a key role in the transfer of the life code into the more organized and complex system of cells. Each cell is like small universe with a central sun.

On a larger, more universal scale, we are tied to the earth, which has its own sun. Furthermore, the earth is tied to the Milky Way, which is tied to other galaxies, and on and on in an infinity of interconnectedness. Now it is easier to understand why all energy and all vibrations penetrate everything, including us.

So who are we? What are we? Are we only bodies, that hold a seat in a spaceship called earth? Or are we a part of something bigger? Philosophers and mystics have been absorbed with these questions through out all time. But again what are we?

I would *like* to know the answer to that question, but I do not *need* to know the answer because I believe that there must be a master plan behind our evolution. I think that physically and mentally, human beings have almost reached perfection in our time.

But what about our spiritual evolution? Since everything revolves around balance, there must be a balance between the physical, mental, and spiritual human being. Why have we forgotten how to charge ourselves with energy in our pursuit to become perfect? This is especially important because the purest form of energy is spiritual energy.

Where do we replenish our energy in today's society? At kindergarten, at school, at university? We might want to look around. Society always reflects "the condition of the empire."

Nowadays there are many people who feel empty and lonely in their existence. But hope is growing and evolving with the advent of environmental groups and everything alternative, from medicine to food. These groups are the foundation for the next generation. We all wish that the world will be a bit different and that our children will inherit a better earth than the one we have helped to create. We have to find a balance for humanity to survive. We have to become more open to spiritual values. We have to build on the Master's words, "man does not live on bread alone."

What Is Light?

"At the end of the rainbow is a pot of gold." For generations children have been told this, if they ask where a rainbow ends. The story about the great flood and Noah's ark is also a symbolic rainbow story. God created a rainbow, which s/he said would appear after each rainfall, as a pledge of her/his promise to not let the world

What Is Light

flood again. The rainbow has become a symbol of the link between God and people. In fact, it is only when we see the rainbow that we truly gain insight into the world of colours. Usually we just think of the world as composed of water and light.

Is light's only function to help us see? No. The light flowing through our eyes helps to trigger hormone production, which influences our entire complex biochemical system. This biochemical system then affects our emotional states.

It is hard to believe that light travels at the speed of 300,000 kilometres per second. The sun is 150 million kilometres away and it takes only 8.5 minutes for light to reach us. Light covers huge distances in a very short time, and it does not travel alone. As you can see in this chart, light travels with other energies.

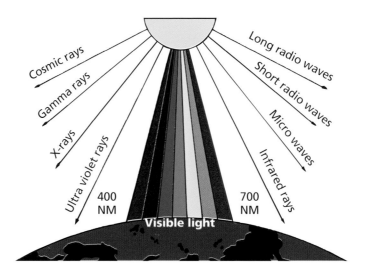

Light wavelengths are between 400 and 700 nanometres. A nanometre (NM) is a millionth of a millimetre or a billionth of a metre and is a standard expression for shortwaves. Gamma rays and x-rays have wavelengths shorter than 400 NM. Micro waves and radio waves have waves longer than 700 NM. Light reaches us via wavelengths and frequencies. Frequencies are often spoken about in Hertz. Both wavelengths and frequencies travel the same distance per minute. Sunlight, which contains all wavelengths, consists of the entire electromagnetic spectrum that we depend on to exist on this planet. It is odd that scientists who understand rays in the atmosphere do not understand the effect that colours have on us.

What Is Light

We know that some rays can be dangerous if we are exposed to them. But the visible light, the rainbow, has a soothing effect on us. This life-giving light can probably give us even more help if we learn to understand what the colours mean.

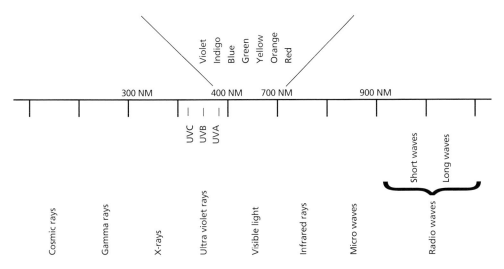

Visible light represents only a small part of electromagnetic waves (EM waves). Other light waves are found beyond red light. And we find ultraviolet on the other side of violet. Modern science and medicine use a variety of waves, from radio and television to microwaves and x-rays. By taking an x-ray, we can look into the physical body without having to operate.

We use radium to help heal cancer. Medical science now also uses other and shorter waves to heal diseases. Ultraviolet light has been used for healing T-cell leukemia. Ultraviolet rays have also been used to kill bacteria. We know that ultraviolet light is important in preventing rickets, as it is a source of vitamin D. We can actually see ultraviolet light, which lies close to the violet light. Medical science claims that the ultraviolet frequencies—well, actually the whole spectrum of visible light—has no medical importance. It is almost unbelievable that the use of all the other rays and waves is accepted, while the properties of visible light are ignored. A human being needs at least twenty to sixty minutes of sunlight every day. The light is absorbed through the eyes and the skin. This short time is enough to maintain the vitamin D level for calcium metabolism. This is essential for the prevention of bone brittleness, which is caused by a lack of calcium. Depression can be caused by a lack of melatonin; and melatonin deficiency is often caused by lack of light. Melatonin deficiency can be prevented by exposing oneself to a full spectrum of light. All colours are present in a full spectrum of light. A full spectrum of light also prevents insomnia.

What Is Light

Sunlight travels 150 million kilometres through empty space until it hits the atmosphere, which is a type of gigantic filter. The top layer of the atmosphere is composed of ozone gases, which filter the strong, energetic, and harmful UV rays. The UVA rays lie just after the violet at 400 NM. The UVA rays go from 400 to 325 NM and the UVB rays from 315 to 280 NM. UVC rays come after that. Less than 1 percent of the sun's waves shorter than 320 NM reach the earth. No rays shorter than 285 NM reach the earth. All rays that have wavelengths above 900 NM will be absorbed by water evaporation. And those that have longer wavelengths are absorbed by carbon dioxide. We receive light all the time, whether it is sunny or cloudy, and the intensity is practically the same.

Ultraviolet light is absorbed by the skin and the eyes. One third of the ultraviolet rays reaching earth are filtered by water and ozone. When the ozone layer absorbs UVC, the rays seldom reach the earth. UVB rays are also filtered, but it depends more on the ozone concentration. Our bodies filter UVA rays through the skin by a pigment called melanin. Each of us is born with a certain amount of melanin. The more melanin you have, the darker your skin colour and the more you can take the sun.

Another light that is very important to us is invisible light, the ultraviolet light at 400-315 NM and the UVB at 315-280 NM. These frequencies have more energy than violet light. These rays determine how we receive the light. We feel good when the sun shines and we stay outside and suntan. We feel beautiful when our skin gets a glow and becomes darker as a result of the UV rays. These rays cause a chemical reaction in the skin that results in vitamin D. You will not find vitamin D in foods other than fish, cod-liver oil, and egg yolks. In Canada and the United States, a plant substitute for vitamin D is added to milk. This is banned in Europe because of the fear of harmful effects of vitamin D in large doses.

> *Vitamin D supplements are extremely important for children living in the northern parts of the world, especially during the winter months. Cod-liver oil is one of the best sources of vitamin D.*

You probably know that a sunburn does more than burn your skin. UV rays can be harmful to our genetic code—the DNA molecules that are found in every cell. Damaged DNA molecules will try to reestablish, but unfortunately they will never be the same. You can therefore gradually destroy your genetic code by getting too much UV light.

What Is Light

The ozone layer surrounding the earth has always protected us from receiving too much of the strong and vital ultraviolet rays. Many people believe that within the last couple of years the ozone layer has been reduced by approximately 2 percent of its original level. So far, this thin layer of ozone has been effective enough in protecting us. Ozone depletion and its harmful effects on people are a controversial issue. It might come to a point when the usually healing and vital ultraviolet rays start to harm people, plants, and animals. And what do we do then? We cannot make everything that lives wear sunglasses and sunscreen with Paba.

I feel very concerned by these alarming projections. We have started to use a new phrase, "lack of light," because indoor artificial light either does not produce or else produces very little of ultraviolet rays. We have different artificial forms of light–white incandescent bulbs which produces light from the red and infrared side of the light spectrum, and neon tubes which produce light in different colour spectra. True light is natural outdoor light from the sun. Ninety-eight percent of natural light is daylight. This light also exposes the natural and true colours of things outdoors.

Several attempts have been made to find out if artificial light is harmful to people. We are affected by chemical pollution in our food, water, and air. Today most food items, from chickens to salad, are grown under artificial light. Do we know what kinds of light energy are used? Is violet, red, blue, or yellow light used? We know from experiments that the growth of vegetables is increased considerably by exposing them to different kinds of light. But do we know if the nutritional value is the same? What do plants do with the artificial light? Does artificial light harm the vitamins and minerals? One thing is sure: it would be wise to be outside as much as you can within the time frames advised.

For more that 5000 years Chinese medicine has recognized the importance of light and its daily and yearly cycles. Light cycles affect our body rhythms and how we sleep, feel, and act. Light also affects the menstrual cycle and feelings during puberty.

Currently a great deal of research is being done on the effects of natural and artificial light on plants and animals. On the leading edge of this research is the Environmental Health and Light Research Institute in Sarasota, Florida, founded by John Ott. John Ott used to be a photographer for Walt Disney Studios, but now he is a photo-biologist. Based on his experiments, John Ott has concluded that a certain quality of light, absorbed through the eyes, can have healing effects on both animals and people. He found that the pigment in the human retina (the cell that determines eye colour) is very sensitive to light and that it is attached to the endocrine system through the pineal and pituitary glands. The path of light into our bodies is very sensitive to the long waves of ultraviolet light.

A Few Hints On How To Absorb The Sun's Energy Properly

SUNLIGHT
Try to be in the sun for at least an hour a day, unless of course the ozone layer gets thinner and we receive more harmful UVB or UVC rays. Take off your glasses and contacts, if you can, but do not look up at the sun.

SUNGLASSES
If you wear sunglasses, make sure they have gray lenses. The neutral gray colour will reduce and balance the light better than the other colours. Other coloured lenses can be harmful for the eyes.

GLASSES
If you wear contacts, use gray coloured lenses. Brown and pink coloured contacts are the worst you can use. Use glasses and contacts that will give you a full spectrum of alternative light.

WINDOW GLASS
Install glass in your home that does not filter UV rays, if you can. But do this only if the ozone layer does not get thinner and if the concentration of harmful UV rays does not increase.

SUNSCREEN
There has been a lot of information and discussion lately about suntan lotions and their harmful effects. This is good news because there are many sunscreens that have Paba in them. Paba blocks ultraviolet rays. We have to think about how we live in this day and age. We live in houses, which block the ultraviolet rays totally. We wear glasses, contacts, and sunglasses, which all block the UV light. We drive cars in which the windows are UV protected, and we work in offices where we are not exposed to UV light either. And when we finally get out into the sun, we put on UV-filter sunglasses, and cover ourselves with sunscreen that also screens out UV rays. We forget that UV rays are a part of the sun's natural rays. And we totally forget that ultraviolet rays contribute to our well-being; they may even be the most important thing for our entire existence.

LIGHT AND VITAMIN D

Sunlight penetrates our bodies through our eyes and skin. The light makes the skin develop the pigment melanin, which stores and helps the skin absorb vitamin D. Vitamin D plays an important role for the body in absorbing calcium, which is essential for bone development. Nowadays, incredible numbers of people suffer from depression, fatigue, lethargy, reduced sex drive, lack of concentration, and headaches. These symptoms are typical reactions to a lack of light. They are found especially in countries with polar nights half of the year. Women from Eastern countries who have moved to northern climates are especially susceptible, because they are heavily clothed and not much light reaches their bodies.

How Do We Absorb Colours Through Light?

1. First, photons reach the retina where they are transformed into electric nerve impulses.
2. These nerve impulses are transferred to the brain through a progressive series of electrochemical reactions in the nerve cells.
3. Finally the back end of the brain receives the electricity and transfers it to the picture we see outside our bodies.

I have not been able to include everything about light and the effect it has on us, but there are many good and instructive books about the subject, some of which I have recommended at the back of this book.

WHO AND WHAT IS GOD?

We all have our own belief in what is guiding us. We have the freedom to choose what we want to believe. But it would be very hard for me to write about colour energies without telling you what I have built my beliefs on. It has to do with the connection between colour energies and body, soul, and thought. God: I think this word contains the essence of energy. This word is charged with so many positive and negative connotations. People have used this word and written stories with so much suffering and wickedness that, to a large degree, it has become associated with negative vibrations.

As people, we have created our own story. We have to take responsibility for the way we have used our knowledge and understanding of the Heavenly Powers, which have created all life. You cannot blame the God-energy for every wrong interpretation. We are all familiar with the word "God." The word "God" means, for most of us, something that does not live on this earth, something intangible, something superior. Some say our Father in Heaven, others say the Lord. I believe that God can be found everywhere. S/he is in me too. I am a part of God and God is a part of me.

The Bible says, "We have been given all the power between heaven and earth." How we use it is up to us. I believe that we have access to unlimited energy. If we use the energy in a positive way and improve ourselves as people, we will leave this earth with positively charged energy. The soul will take this experience, the positive energy, with it when it leaves the body at death. The work continues–it gathers more positive energy when it is reincarnated back on earth. This energy will again be created and transformed by another person, who develops characteristics and transforms acts into spiritual thoughts, which again are energies. When the soul has gathered enough energy from the earth, it continues its development in heaven. In heaven, it also improves itself until all the energy has become clean, pure, white energy–God's energy. This energy is never bigger, whiter, or purer than the soul's development. God is pure energy, and we, as God's children, are here to learn how to develop this energy. We use this energy when we pray and ask for help. We draw God's power down to us. And what is God's power other than the power we give off through our lives?

Generations before us have contributed to this power source, and we have to do the same. Our descendants will reap the fruits of our efforts. They must draw on God's power. That is why what we do today in our lives is so important. God is pure energy, and we have to choose whether we want to use this energy positively or negatively in our thinking and behaviour.

Many sects and religious and nonreligious groups have tried to find answers to questions about God, life, and death. There are no problems as long as they respect each other's attempts to figure it all out, and as long as they understand that basically there is only one answer, one energy, one God. God is the word all our efforts arise from. The word "God" has produced messengers–Buddha, Jesus, Mohammed, Baha'u'llah, and others–and they have all caused people to develop spiritually.

A great many people await the next spiritual messenger. Perhaps there will not be another–so far, we have not received them very well.

2

THE HISTORY OF COLOUR AND ENERGY

During the past two hundred years, four men in particular fought for the same idea that the colour energy of light could be beneficially utilized.

	born	died
Baron Karl von Reichenbach	1788	1869
Dr. Edwin Babbitt	1829	1905
John Keely	1837	1898
Dr. Wilhelm Reich	1897	1957

Baron Karl von Reichenbach was a businessman and chemist who discovered paraffin and creosote. He was also a qualified metallurgist and an expert on meteorites. His main interest, however, was in the vital force he called the Odic Force. Reichenbach discovered that everything gives off a light. He described this phenomenon by saying "We live in a world where everything shines and vibrates."

Around the same time, Dr. Edwin Babbitt, in America, heard about Reichenbach's work. Babbitt was an artist, mystic, doctor, and clairvoyant. His book *The Principle of Light and Color* is a classic essay on the subject. He invented an apparatus he called the Chromolume. He would suspend coloured glass in a window so that the sun could shine through the glass and down onto a patient. This method has been used by many people since then, but now usually with artificial light.

John Keely lived at about the same time as Babbitt. He was more of a theorist. His theory was that the atmosphere contained endless elements of energy, which he called cosmic particles. He believed that their different vibrations could be isolated and then stored or converted into usable energy sources–for car engines, for example. He called the different parts of these cosmic particles, vibro molecules, vibro atoms, and vibro force. Keely discovered that he could make a small, light model airplane fly freely in a room by playing a certain note on a violin. Keely worked day and night on various other projects, and many business people invested money in his experiments. Keely knew that he was on to something big, something which would revolutionize the world–but unfortunately his investors lost their patience. They seized his papers, which they did not understand. Sadly, Keely died in poverty without any of his ideas being realized. There has been a book written about his theories called *Keely and His Discoveries*.

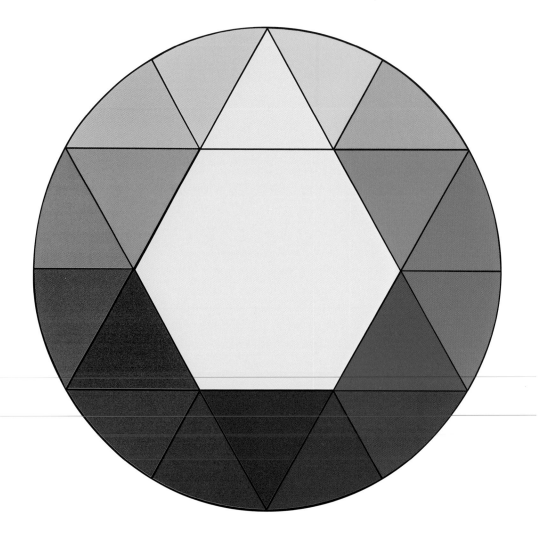

The History Of Colour And Energy

Austrian-born Wilhelm Reich studied at the University of Vienna and worked in the field of neuro-psychiatry. His theories did not find favour in Europe, and in the 1930's he moved to America. Reich discovered an energy, which he called Orgon. Reich believed that this energy (also known as chi, prana, od, the ruling power, or life energy) was the universal life-force and that it vitalized everything–plants, minerals, animals, birds, and people. Reich built an instrument–the Orgonscope –which allowed him to observe this energy. The Orgonscope was an adult size box made of layered organic and inorganic materials. This box was to be used outdoors, and the temperature inside the box was significantly higher than outside of it. If someone lay in the box, s/he would tan even without direct sunlight. Cuts, wounds, and other injuries would heal faster and painlessly when the accumulated energy from the box was focused on the injured areas.

Reich devised other experiments with this energy. He invented a device that could be used to affect the weather. In the Arizona desert, he made clouds produce rain. Reich also worked with radioactivity and, like Keely, dabbled in the subject of energy for engine power. But this subject was so frightening, with all its possibilities and problems, that he never put anything down on paper. Reich believed that if this secret fell into the hands of the wrong people, it could be the end of the human race. The Vedic books of India say "a yogi who has full control over prana can move an atom or a planet with his willpower." When you think about it, it is probably a good thing that Reich kept the information secret. Unfortunately later in his life, during a trial, he was convicted of contempt of court. All his papers and his laboratory were destroyed. His books were burned and his own writings were prevented from being reprinted. Lastly, he was imprisoned for two years without access to writing material.

Madame Blavatsky, a leader in metaphysics during the late 1800's, commented that people were not ready for Reich's knowledge and so they presented continual obstacles in his path as he pursued his theories. It must have been strange for Reich to hold the key to a universal secret and yet be powerless to do anything with it.

Other thinkers and scientists have also written about the relationship between light and energy. Isaac Newton's *Optics*, published in 1704, is the foundation of today's knowledge of light and the colour spectrum. Newton used a prism to investigate the seven light energies–red, orange, yellow, green, blue, indigo, and violet–that can be seen in a rainbow. The importance of this discovery was that the spectrum now could be seen with the naked eye. The spectrum can also be seen through a raindrop or dewdrop when the sun shines through it.

The History Of Colour And Energy

Johann Wolfgang von Goethe published his *Colour Teachings* in 1808. His writings on colour are almost as popular as his literary work *Faust*. Goethe's theory about colours is an invaluable tool for everyone who works with colours. I highly recommend Goethe's *Colour Teachings* if you are particularly interested in colours and colour combinations.

In 1877, Dr. S. Pancoast published a paper entitled, *Blue and Red Light and Its Rays as Medicine*. It is primarily about red and blue rays and their respective stimulating and calming effects on people.

Danish physicist Niels Rydberg-Finsen (1860-1904), a Nobel Prize winner for medicine, is another well-known scholar. He was internationally famous for his work with light and colours. In 1893 he published a paper on the use of light in medicine. He proved that ultraviolet radiation has enormous biological effects, and could be used to treat tuberculosis and smallpox. Rydberg-Finsen founded a light institute for the treatment of skin tuberculosis. He also used light to treat smallpox and discovered a way to reduce smallpox scarring by using red light rays.

Albert Szent-Gyorgi, a Nobel Prize winner who discovered vitamin C, developed the idea that all the energy absorbed by our bodies comes, ultimately, from the sun. By studying photosynthesis, he noted how the sun's energy is stored in plants, which are, in turn, eaten by humans and animals. In this way the energy of the sun is passed on and used as energy in our bodies.

Light, Colours, And Colour Tests

Max Lüscher, a Swiss psychology professor, is probably the best-known contemporary authority on the use of colour to analyze personalities. Some twenty years ago, Lüscher developed a colour test as a method of mapping out different personalities. Another well-known author on colour, is Britain's Theo Gimbel. Gimbel was a student of Rudolf Steiner. He has written on the subject of the stimulating effect of red on under-active people and the calming effects of blue on aggressive personalities.

Two other important works are *Know Yourself Through Color* by Marie Louise Lacy and *Colour Your Life* by Dorothy and Howard Sun. Both books include colour tests which analyze different personalities. Another influential person is

Karl Ryberg. Ryberg has a clinic in Sweden that uses colour-light therapy. He uses monochromatic laser light in his treatment of psychosomatic illnesses. He also wrote a book called *Living Colours*. I am sure in our time many more people will influence history in the development of light, energy, and colour theories.

WHAT IS A CHAKRA?

The idea of chakras is taken from an ancient system of yoga. The word chakra is derived from Sanskrit and means literally "wheel" or "plate," but it generally implies an energy wheel. There are seven main chakras, which are centred approximately in the middle of our bodies. They are tied to the nervous system along the spine, the endocrine system, and various glands. The chakras are also linked to various bodily functions such as breathing and digestion.

The chakras basically represent the four elements–earth, water, fire, and air–as well as sound, light, and thought. Each chakra is represented by one of the seven colours of the rainbow–red, orange, yellow, green, blue, indigo, and violet. Stones, minerals, music, herbs, and plants are also linked to the chakras.

The seven colour energies, though, are the prime power behind every chakra. Every chakra has a latent "mission" or "assignment" that has to be fulfilled. Moreover, the fulfillment of these missions is a birthright of every individual. Unfortunately, life is filled with so many unforeseen incidents that it can be difficult for a person to fulfill these needs and still remain balanced and positive. We have a right to fulfill the mission or inherent need associated with each chakra.

The Red Root Centre–The Right "To Have"

The right to survive is the most important aspect of the red energy centre. Food, clothing, shelter, heat, medical aid, and physical contact are among the most important things in life. Concern with these basics is a primary part of the red energy, and it will always seek a way to best satisfy these needs. If it does not succeed on the positive side, the negative side will react.

What Is A Chakra?

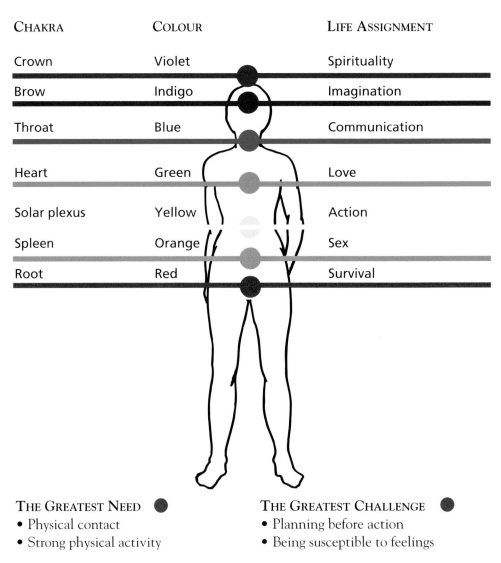

CHAKRA	COLOUR	LIFE ASSIGNMENT
Crown	Violet	Spirituality
Brow	Indigo	Imagination
Throat	Blue	Communication
Heart	Green	Love
Solar plexus	Yellow	Action
Spleen	Orange	Sex
Root	Red	Survival

THE GREATEST NEED
- Physical contact
- Strong physical activity

THE GREATEST CHALLENGE
- Planning before action
- Being susceptible to feelings

The Orange Spleen Centre–The Right "To Feel"

Accusations like "shame on you" or "you have no right to be angry" are very hard on orange energy, as it does not like to be told what to feel. It is very hard for the orange energy to know what it wants to *do* if it is not allowed to *feel* freely.

THE GREATEST NEED
- To be respected and acknowledged, especially by family and friends

THE GREATEST CHALLENGE
- To achieve a deeper contact with oneself
- To be oneself and give love to others

The Yellow Solar Plexus Centre–The Right "To Act"

We are trained to obey and submit to authority from childhood. Parents who use their power to raise "good" children, and teachers or other authorities who demand blind obedience, block the yellow child's personal willpower and the ability to express themselves freely.

THE GREATEST NEED
- To live in an organized world where everything is orderly and disciplined
- To be an intellectual individualist
- To understand what is read or studied

THE GREATEST CHALLENGE
- To follow one's heart
- To work without conflicts

The Green Heart Centre–The Right "To Love And Be Loved"

People need to love. Emotional blockages arise when people are exposed to racial discrimination, cultural barriers, and war. These things block love out. Furthermore, the heart chakra can simply close if you do not receive enough love as a child or as an adult.

THE GREATEST NEED
- To feel protected
- To love and be loved
- To have hidden resources

THE GREATEST CHALLENGE
- To love without reservations
- To control greed
- To be able to control fear and insecurity

The Blue Throat Centre–The Right "To Talk And Live In Truth"

Messages such as "do not talk like that" or "calm down if you are that angry!" stop us from expressing our feelings. This suppression of feelings can lead to the closing of the throat chakra. Our throat chakra will also close when we have to listen to family lies, or keep secrets that we do not wish to keep.

THE GREATEST NEED
- To live an ideal life
- To be surrounded by beauty and peace
- To have control over one's mental abilities

THE GREATEST CHALLENGE
- To live more spontaneously
- To take more risks
- To find the truth about oneself instead of finding faults in others

The Indigo Brow Centre–The Right "To See" ●

Your forehead chakra can close when someone tries to tell you that what you see or think is not real, when someone lies and keeps things hidden from you, and when the development of your "third eye" is hampered.

THE GREATEST NEED ●
- To feel at one with the universe
- To be a part of strengthening human development

THE GREATEST CHALLENGE ●
- To turn vision into reality
- To develop the five senses extraordinarily

The Violet Crown Centre–The Right "To Know" ●

Restraint can, paradoxically, really inspire a violet person. By taking away a violet person's opportunity to develop spiritually or to spread spiritual knowledge, or by subjecting a violet person to dictatorial forces, extra spiritual energy is generated, and this is what creates saints.

THE GREATEST NEED ●
- To feel at one with the universe
- To feel that everything in life has a purpose

THE GREATEST CHALLENGE ●
- To be able to relay the "big" inspiration to other people

The development of these characteristics or natural demands happens throughout our life. Since each chakra is receiving and rearranging information all the time it is important to understand the positive and negative characteristics of all the chakras, and to go back through your own life to see if you remember incidents that could have affected the development of the chakras. Each chakra has a special meaning in the growing and aging process:

THE RED CHAKRA: *birth to nine months.*
THE ORANGE CHAKRA: *six months to two years.*
THE YELLOW CHAKRA: *eighteen months to three years.*
THE GREEN CHAKRA: *three years to six years.*
THE BLUE CHAKRA: *six years to ten years.*
THE INDIGO CHAKRA: *seven years to twelve years.*
THE VIOLET CHAKRA: *twelve years on.*

Blockages In The Energy Centres

Different experiences throughout our lives can create blockages in our chakras. A child, for example, who is hit by a parent quickly learns the need to control his or her body to prevent being hit again. A child who does not receive enough love and attention learns how to shut out emotional needs. Noise, pollution, depressing surroundings, and stress can affect our health and block the chakras. The energy centres, however, can be trained to open and close, just like muscles. This is complicated work, so do not rush it; you need to develop your knowledge of the energy centres and to understand their untapped potential. It is an exciting way of training your conscious self.

The Red Chakra–The Root Energy

The first energy centre, which is red, represents our roots, our foundation, and our survival. The centre's main assignment is to create a safe and strong foundation, which can help the other energy centres when they need it. If your red power station is strong, your body will also be healthy, strong, and steady, and it will give you strength for the other assignments. In chakra terminology, this centre is called the Mudlahara, which means "root." The assignment for the root centre is to keep you in touch with the ground; think of a tree which requires deep roots to gather strength from the earth so that its branches can grow high. People we call "down to earth" who have their "feet firmly planted on the ground" have strong root energy centres.

Early Affects On The Red Chakra

A prospective mother usually tries to do the right things during pregnancy such as taking prenatal vitamins and avoiding harmful medication. Since the root centre is greatly influenced by how we feel, a woman's attitude toward her pregnancy will influence the kind of energy passed on to the fetus. A difficult birth can cause trauma, making it tough for the child to access his or her physical body in later years. The root chakra can also be damaged if the infant is separated from the mother for long periods of time immediately after birth. The mother/child connection, developed through breastfeeding and intimate contact, is essential to establish a strong root centre. The use of sedatives at the time of birth can also affect the root chakra by weakening a child's instincts, making her or him apathetic and listless.

In the very beginning, the child's centre is concentrated around survival. Hunger, warmth, comfort, and the need to feel attached to the mother are essential. Blockages will occur later in life if some of this basic level of comfort is missing or is not satisfactory.

Our physical universe starts with our body, and one thing is sure: we only get this one body from birth till death. I cannot emphasize this enough: the body is the home of the soul and the foundation for our entire life on earth. Thanks to our body we can see and understand everything that happens within us. When we are sick or in trouble our body lets us know. What we cannot control by knowledge and will is expressed through our bodies in the form of abscesses and sores, stiff joints, and sore muscles. We have to learn to be in contact with and respect our bodies and our root centres.

Thoughts

Thoughts can trigger emotional changes, from calmness to anger. When this happens adrenaline is increased, blood vessels contract, and blood pressure becomes higher. We also breathe faster, our hearts pound, and we get muscle pains in our stomachs. These changes, in turn, trigger an increase of endocrine secretions and fluids from the adrenal and thyroid glands. The pituitary gland also plays an important role, as it helps to release hormones, which both stimulate and calm the adrenal and thyroid glands.

Actions are closely connected to our thoughts and to the energy that flows in and out of the crown chakra. Hormones, which are influenced by our thoughts, control our physical expression of feelings. This confirms the physiological principle that energy follow thought. Ultimately one could say that there is an integral, vital connection between the seven chakras, the seven colours, the endocrine glands, and the seven stages of consciousness.

> *All chakras send out energy in the form of rays. If the energy you send out is negative, then that's what will come back to you. You might notice that you have bad experiences after you have had negative thoughts. You wonder why everyone is so angry with you, when you feel you have done nothing wrong. But the truth is that* YOU *are at fault: your own negativity has returned to you. Feelings between people are forms of positive or negative thoughts, which hang like a carpet of fog around the people in question. I am sure that we all know how wonderful it feels to be in a positive cloud and how awful it feels to be in a negative cloud. You must realize how often it is your own thoughts that cause a positive or negative flow of feelings between people. It is not just what you say that counts, but what you think as well. What you think is the most important consideration. Your negative thoughts will eventually cause you harm. You must either change your way of thinking or remove yourself from the causes of these negative thoughts.*

WHAT IS COLOUR ENERGY?

Light is energy; colour comes from light; the result is energy from colours or colour energy. Colour Energy has developed a system which makes it easier to understand how to obtain these energy-resources, which lie in the colours just waiting to be used. The body's power station has the energy and vitality we need, but most of us do not know how to tap into it.

Who would not like to have unlimited energy to act, think, be understood, and feel with more vitality and happiness? It's possible if you want it but you have to really want it. The energy comes out of the "will" that is used to carry out a lot of daily rituals. There is no easy way for a person to find their way back to the energy-resources of childhood. The natural happiness and spontaneity of youth supported this flow of unlimited energy. Unfortunately, our energy dissipates as the years go by.

The orange energy is extremely important in developing energy reserves. It is like everything else: every little bit is a part of the whole and the whole is nothing without all the little bits and pieces. We call it a holistic way of thinking.

Nowadays, people think holistically and use holistic therapies. Yet we do not look at our own person and our own energy power station as a holistic whole. We have seven colour energy centres and all of them have to work. It does not do the body any good just to use one talent, even if it is an inherited or naturally positive talent because you are then like a motor with seven cylinders driving on only one cylinder. We were created to use all seven cylinders. The colour energy centres must spin and be in harmony and in balance with each other. Now, how can you achieve this yourself?

We must take stock of ourselves. One way is to make a T-account of your personality and behaviour traits.

On one side of the "T" write down your positive traits and on the other side your negative traits. Look up the negative and positive characteristics under each colour in Chapter 3. If you function more with the negative side of yourself, you must start to align yourself more with the positive. This is important because the negative side leads to illness, decay, and physical death.

WHAT IS THE DIFFERENCE BETWEEN US?

What a colourful sight we are! On the outside, our skin is either white, black, brown, red, or yellow. We can be French, Spanish, Chinese, Aboriginal, or Arab. People may differ in the colour of their skin and in their personal characteristics, but inside we are all more or less the same. For as long as the world has been turning, people have not changed the way they express the positive and negative aspects of themselves. Our negative characteristics include anger, fear, cowardliness, laziness, slyness, craftiness, and falseness. And on the positive side there is joy, happiness, love, charity, kindness, and helpfulness. The list of good and bad characteristics does come to an end though. Ultimately this is all that we can know, develop, learn, think, and do. There are no more expressions for our positive and negative qualities. Let us have a look at the T-account again. On one side the positive, and the other the negative.

With everything there is a balance. When you have a positive side, you must also have a negative side. The ultimate consequence of looking at the positive and negative sides of yourself is that you can look objectively at the two sides of yourself, the kind and good self and the wicked and bad self. If it is a happy and cheerful characteristic trait on the positive side, then it must be a sad and miserable trait on the negative side. Or if it is a wise and intelligent personalitiy trait on the positive side, it must be a dumb and dimwitted trait on the other side.

POSITIVE	NEGATIVE

What Is The Difference Between Us?

We live most of our lives in a balance zone. At times we tip over to the negative zone. We have to remember that we are not creatures with hidden qualities that no other creatures have. There are no depths or unknown sources from where a person can pick up shapes and feelings that nobody else has. Imagine if this were you:

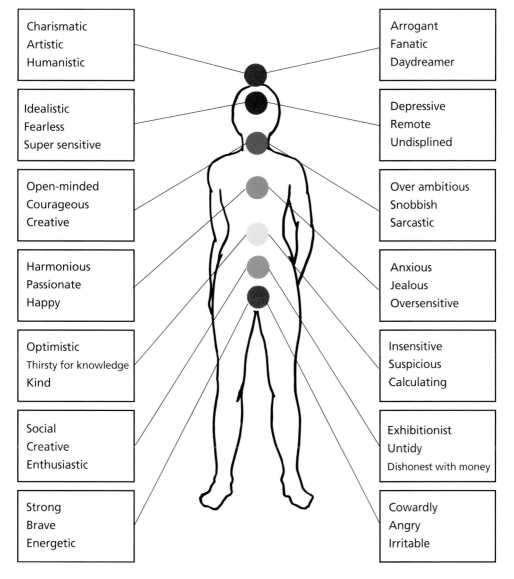

POSITIVE

NEGATIVE

Positive	Negative
Charismatic, Artistic, Humanistic	Arrogant, Fanatic, Daydreamer
Idealistic, Fearless, Super sensitive	Depressive, Remote, Undisplined
Open-minded, Courageous, Creative	Over ambitious, Snobbish, Sarcastic
Harmonious, Passionate, Happy	Anxious, Jealous, Oversensitive
Optimistic, Thirsty for knowledge, Kind	Insensitive, Suspicious, Calculating
Social, Creative, Enthusiastic	Exhibitionist, Untidy, Dishonest with money
Strong, Brave, Energetic	Cowardly, Angry, Irritable

What Is The Difference Between Us?

Here are a few guidelines. I do not believe that anybody can stay on one side of themselves only. That is, you cannot know your positive side without knowing your negative side. When a person understands and admits that s/he has not only a positive side but also a negative side, s/he can then see themselves as a whole person. It then becomes difficult to see other people as strangers. Every person has seven energy centres that contains positive and negative possibilities.

Everybody has access to the same energy sources, but the energy has the potential to be used negatively. The energy is the same, but you are the one who decides how to use it. This is the reason why I say that people are so alike. We have access to the same energy, but one person can use it in a negative way, and another person in a positive way.

Your personality, which makes you different from other people, is a mix of your main colour energy and how the six other colour energies are distributed on your colour scale. It is easy to recognize the almost automatic behaviour of a red person when s/he is on the negative side. The same goes for the blue person's negative traits of arrogance, sarcasm, and extreme self-confidence. The positive blue traits are thoughtfulness and understanding. We only have a certain amount of energy to squander; nothing more or less than what the seven people types and seven energy sources can give us. Because of this, it should not be too hard to understand each other. We can know a lot about another people when we know where the balance is between positive and negative characteristics, and which colour the energy belongs to.

When a problem arises and you are facing someone who does not understand your point of view, you really have to be careful and think about the nature of that person's energy. What energy is affecting the way s/he talks, acts and understands? Is s/he an emotional person or someone driven by willpower? Is s/he in balance or is the negative side more dominant? If you recognize that whatever energy or qualities this individual is displaying are identical to your own energy and characteristics, then you will be in a better position to understand this person.

Have you ever met someone that you really disliked and wanted to avoid? You might dismiss them, thinking they are just not your "type." This is a potentially explosive situation–something has happened in the past, something buried deep in our memories and feelings, that makes us react this way. Your "indigo" intuitive energy may be warning you about as past karmic conflict–perhaps this individual you dislike is the reincarnation of a soul that had once done battle with your soul, or maybe this individual is triggering memories or unresolved problems from your present life. Perhaps you did not complete your assignment, or chose to forget it. Your body and the brain that stores your life's data have not forgotten though, and this person may have helped to activate the body's memory, allowing these feelings to surface. It would be wise and healthy for you to find out why you are reacting the way you do. If you can learn to understand your own memories and experiences and why you do not like a particular person, you essentially become your own therapist. If you cannot figure your responses out, then consider going to a therapist, preferably one who works with emotional and physical blockages, perhaps through acupuncture or polarity therapy.

The following is a summary of the main points discussed so far:

There is no one who is different from you.

Other people just use different energies than you.

People use positive and negative energies.

You know all the energies.

You know the positive and negative sides of each energy.

You can understand other people.

Before we start to look at each separate colour energy, ask yourself some questions: "Am I a dreamer? Do I live in a fantasy world? Am I an athletic person? Am I an intellectual?"

On page 44 is a question with seven possible answers. Tick off the answer that describes you the most. Then read the Chapter 3, which describes the seven colours and their energies. Make sure you complete the readings about all the colours, before you form an opinion about which colour best describes yourself. After reading about all the colours, you can then decide which colour describes you and what kind of person you are the best. Then check with page 117 to compare the colour you have chosen with your answer to the question on page 44.

WHAT IS MOST IMPORTANT TO YOU?

☐ 1. Your body and what you can see, touch, smell, taste and hear. Your sex life and physical goals.

☐ 2. Your relationships with friends. Meeting new interesting people. Good food and drink in good company.

☐ 3. Your intellectual life. Your interesting studies. Your interesting work. Good team work.

☐ 4. Economic security. Your family. Sharing happiness. A nice home.

☐ 5. Peace and order. Your ability to manage and organize. Seeing things clearly and planning for the future. Your need to see beauty around you all the time.

☐ 6. Your ability to understand something you have never learned, seen, or heard before. Your strong belief in "something" within yourself. Your strong and imaginative dreams about the future. Your strong belief that you have an inner strength helping you.

☐ 7. Your incredible ability to come up with new ideas. Your wish to write, paint, and compose to express the way you feel. Your ability to feel a spiritual inspiration in everything that exists. Your ability to be driven or inspired by a higher power.

3

WHAT COLOUR ARE YOU?

We are going to get a little bit more personal now and examine the colours to see if we can recognize their qualities in ourselves and in others. Nobody is only one colour. We are all a rainbow of colours. Some of us use more of the earthy colours, such as red, yellow, and orange. Others use more of the airy violet, indigo, and blue energy. What makes us different is that we all use different colour "fuel." Generally, the energy we use to think and act with is a direct result of the energy we absorb.

The type of energy we use the most helps to define our personalities and individual characteristics. Furthermore, we are born on this planet with reincarnated souls that carry information from past lives which also shapes our personality. Cosmic energy influences from other planets and hereditary genes are contributing factors as well. All these elements play an important part in why we have different personalities. By taking our colour test at the end of the book you will find out which main energy you rely on, as well as the order of the other six energies. This will tell you who you are and which type of energy you use the most–if it is willpower or emotional energy. It is not absolutely necessary to take the test to find out about your positive and negative sides. If you know yourself well, you can use the T-account system as previously explained. But the test is very helpful and can give you a better and more objective opinion regarding the energy you use most.

Read about all the colour energies and how they are expressed positively and negatively. Figure out which colour dominates your personality. It will be great to know who you are and why you react as you do in different situations. You will get a better understanding of yourself and others–the world will become easier to live in when you understand how alike, and yet still so different we are.

Before you read about the different colour energies, try to guess what colour best describes you. Do you think you are red or violet, etc. Write it down. It will be fun to see what you intuitively thought, before you learned what the colours mean.

I think I am _____

Red people ~
Red sex ~ Red health ~ Money
and success for red people ~ Occupations
for red people ~ Red children ~ Red parents ~
Red relationships ~ Red interior design ~ Red
energy drinks ~ Red gemstones ~ Red food ~
The red centre, organs and glands ~ Affirmations
for red people ~ Red energy, overactive
and underactive ~ Red positive
and negative

RED ENERGY AND
WHY YOU ARE A RED PERSON

Red People

Red people are not abstract thinkers. To them a table is a table. That is it. They feel comfortable in the physical world and throw themselves into the world with absolute confidence and courage. Their strongest quality is their ability to encounter everyday life with inherent security and confidence.

Red people are earthy people who respect the laws of nature and understand their role in the physical world. Red energy also encourages participation. This energy is forceful and vital, like a volcano. If there is an eruption on the positive side, it shows up as involvement in issues such as truth and justice. Red people believe in human causes. They protect those weaker than themselves. They would give their own life to help others. Red people feel pain and physical warnings less than others, but that does not mean that they are less emotional. Like many fruits, the outside is hard but the inside is soft. When red people marry they should marry warm sensitive people who are not afraid to show their feelings. The best partner is often the green type, if they are both balanced. If they are at all interested in their own well-being they ought to marry this type of person.

Society needs red people. They are not afraid to break away from old dogmas and entrenched principles. Their stamina and daring nature is wonderfully refreshing and cleansing. But it is not easy for the red energy to stay in balance. It may be easier to recognize negative red energy, so let's take a look at the negative side of this energy. Red people can easily use their surplus energy in negative ways if they focus too much on their own egos and if they do not use the other colour energies when needed. Negative red people often have had parents who encouraged them as children to stick up for themselves. "Fight back," and "show them who is in charge" are messages that they probably heard many times. Thus, it is easy for them to feel that only the strong can survive and that people are strong if they do not cry or complain. To them life is a dangerous enemy. Nobody can be trusted.

Red Energy And Why You Are A Red Person

Very often they will respond to new ideas or projects in a very negative or discouraging way. This is the opposite of what their positive red energy stands for. To really begin to understand negative red people you must believe that their hardness, outer imbalance, cursing, and aggressive brutality is a façade. Behind all this negativity, there is a little boy or girl who cannot find their balance. The side which is soft and vulnerable is seldom displayed. But if they get married to a green person they will find inner peace.

Whether positively or negatively balanced, red people always take the underdog's side. A society based on bureaucratic authority is not suitable for the straightforward and just red people. Freedom fighters and liberation groups hold a lot of red energy. It can be difficult for other people to understand red energy when it uses power and dissension to get attention. Red people like fights, conflicts, and confrontations. They are straightforward in speech and action and they have difficulty understanding why others do not always appreciate this direct way of speaking. They chase people away with their love of confrontation. What other people see as aggressiveness, they see as contact, conversation, and togetherness. Red people often attack others to find out if the person is honest. Can they be trusted? Who is a friend and who is an enemy? They have to know who they can talk to and socialize with. False and haughty manners do not impress red people. They will often provoke a situation to enable them to see what is hiding behind a person's mask. They need to know who they are dealing with. They will respect an opponent as long as they know what the person stands for. Red people can also be very opinionated. They shut out everybody else's arguments and only see their own solutions. It is as if they believe that if they show trust and kindness, other people's good ideas or vitality will hurt them. This attitude only shows that their biggest weaknesses are their stubbornness and their inability to admit that other people have positive qualities. Red people have to admit that they have a positive side too, in order to find their balance.

Red people prefer physical challenges to emotional or intellectual challenges. They need to feel that there is a purpose to being alive. Consequently, they are good at actualizing ideas. They are not afraid of taking chances or starting businesses. They are born starters. In business transactions they are an essential part of any team. They have natural know-how on how things should develop. Their ability to make an idea become reality is one of their strongest qualities. They do not like to participate in big planning meeting, but give them an idea and they will come back with details on how to develop the project—and they will do it right away. For red people, a project on a piece of paper in the form of words, numbers, and drawings is not worth anything until it is realized.

Red Sex

Red energy contains the biggest wonder of all–the drive for reproduction. It is this drive that creates love, passion, happiness and vitality, not to mention offspring. But it also causes rape, incest, and sexual deviation. Here, as with any other energy, it is unbalance that is the cause. When red energy is balanced positively, the reproduction energy expresses itself through normal sex.

A red person does not need to flirt, or have candlelight, good food, and music to set the stage for sex. No, their urges are more spontaneous. This is not easy for the romantic green person or the sophisticated orange person to understand. The sexual drive is a natural urge that is coloured by the type of lover the red person naturally is. One really has to understand the red energy. The red person has a conquest instinct and a Tarzan-like mentality when it comes to sex. Sex is a natural part of life for the robust red person, and he or she gets a type of animal satisfaction from the red sex act. Sex is one of life's biggest pleasures for the red person. That's why s/he has problems with religions and organizations that believe sex should not be talked about. The red person does not like to feel sinful or to feel something is wrong with his/her feelings or choice when it comes to sex. Red people feel that they should be able to have whatever kind of sex life they want.

Red Health

Red people's health problems are often work related. Red people frequently have high-risk jobs, and if they are not in balance, accidents can happen. Red people are not afraid to lend someone a hand. This is an excellent quality, but they better be in balance otherwise red people will get back problems, sciatica, and lumbago. Red people frequently cut themselves on work-related or household tools. They have to learn how to slow down. Rest is very important for active red people. They need to rest well after hard physical work. They also need to control their appetite for life. A voracious appetite for sex and food can easily shift the red energy's balance to the negative side. The colour red has the longest wavelength of the light spectrum. Red in someone's aura indicates vitality and energy. Red also stimulates and helps the automatic nervous system and the liver.

Health Tips For Red People

This dynamic and sex-productive energy is the slowest of all the colour frequencies in the spectrum. Many people with illnesses need this energy's warmth. Healers with access to red energy can help patients suffering from chronic polyarthritis, rheumatism, lumbago, sciatica, and stiff, sore muscles. Red energy also relieves menstrual pain. If you have problems with being aroused sexually you should wear red underwear. Red sheets or other red items may also help. If you have blood problems, you should drink beet juice or red grapefruit juice.

Money And Success For Red People

Red people are not driven by money. Money is a necessity for survival, but it does not rule their lives. Success is the result of the moment for red people. They want to see the result of their work right away. They flourish in result-oriented jobs.

Occupations For Red People

Red people make good salespeople, politicians, surgeons, wrestlers, boxers, emergency rescue workers, fire fighters, construction workers, carpenters, dancers, and project starters.

Red Children

Red children have independent and strong personalities. They are often stubborn, with fierce tempers. At kindergarten and at school they are usually the ones who start fights. They enjoy the practical subjects the best. Purely philosophical subjects have no interest or meaning for them. They like to receive recognition and admiration for what they have done. All children like to receive praise and hugs, but red children do not want to be praised and hugged in front of other people. They are very result oriented and want to receive a reward right away. There is no point in promising a red child a future reward, because red children only understand the connection between their present actions and what they receive immediately. Parents can help their red children by finding a way for the children to use their strong and natural energy constructively. The children will also have to learn how to deal with their emotions in a relaxed and quiet way. They have to learn how to discuss their feelings so that they do not hold in their aggressions.

Red Male Adolescents

How to properly deal with red adolescent boys is a very confusing issue. Physical and emotional development happens at the same time in the teenage years and can be a very strenuous and powerful process. Boys are becoming young men and are naturally interested in sex. But in today's society there have been many changes in men's roles. Men have had to give up a lot of male attitudes and replace them with more feminine ones. This is good as long as there is a balance between feminine and masculine energies. It is fine if a mother tells her red child to be polite and friendly. But when a mother tries to quiet her son's red restless virility down, she is the one who does not understand. Her red child is not like Ms. Smith's blue son. A red adolescent boy needs to be active and virile. His red energy has to be able to express itself. It is better to give a red boy physical activities that make him physically exhausted than for him to become frustrated. He has to be able to feel proud of his masculinity. He is not going to be a girlfriend to his girlfriends but a guy who is a friend to his girlfriends.

Red Energy And Why You Are A Red Person

There are many differences between red boys and, for example, yellow, blue, and indigo boys. A red boy cannot talk himself into an orgasm. He needs action. Just because a red person has this hunting instinct and wishes to bring down the prey fast, he must not feel that he is violent, raw, uncivilized, crude, or always occupied with sex. He acts the way he does because that is the way the energies work through him. And these energies have the blood's speed and rhythm. It has been proven that many young men have a problem with the new picture of masculinity, and that sperm quality can be reduced by a change in role pattern–that is, when men have to pretend to be something they are not. This pertains to red men in particular, but it is important for all men that they have a balanced root chakra. Primitive forces lie there, and these forces carry life for future generations. We have to be careful not to lump everyone together. We are all different. The red man is a man with a capital M.

Red Parents

Usually children of red parents either fear or admire their parents' physical strength. Red parents are protective and constantly worry about their children. But they can have difficulties communicating with them. They do not like to talk about feelings. They show their affection by playing sports or by physically working with their children. Red parents are good at teaching their children to take pleasure in their work and to understand that you get what you work for. If red parents are unbalanced, they may use physical punishment on their children too much.

Red Relationships

Red people like the togetherness of a relationship. Many people feel attracted to these red bundles of energy. Red people are hard workers and very loyal. They work persistently to provide material things for their homes. They are very grounded realists who can offer partners an easy and practical life. Their strong hot temper creates a fiery personality. Imagine a volcano or a hot spring: the energy is so powerful that it has to come out once in a while. You just have to learn how to ease the pressure.

It can be very exciting to be in a relationship with a balanced red person. But a red person with too much concentrated red energy may turn vulgar, brutal, domineering, arrogant, extremely self-centred, and sexually abusive. With too little red energy, the red person can become cowardly, indecisive, ungrateful, racist, judgmental, and unforgiving.

Red Energy And Why You Are A Red Person

RELATIONSHIPS RED/RED
In this relationship both people are strong-willed and physically robust. They have the same needs, so they understand
each other fully. A problematic situation between two red
people can seem much more difficult and overpowering than it
actually is, so it is not wise to interfere in their discussion. Often they tell each
other the brutal honest truth, because their ability to communicate and to show
their feelings is not their strongest point. They both have strong opinions about
how things should be. They can also be stubborn. When balanced, they are strong
team players and can be a strong couple.

RELATIONSHIPS RED/ORANGE
In this relationship, the two people are strong physically,
but that is where the similarities end. The red person uses
willpower energy, while the orange person uses emotional
energy. The sensitive and emotional orange person is easily dominated by the
strong red person. The red person, on the other hand, can provide stability in the
orange person's life. Since an orange person can often be childlike and indecisive,
the red person can take on a protective and caring role. They both also like physical work and are constantly rearranging their furniture. They both like to work
outside and around the house. Frequently they have the same kind of hobbies or
occupations. The red person is the responsible one in the relationship, and the
orange person is the one who brings laughter and happiness into the life of the
hard-working red person. If in balance, the two people enjoy life together in a
down-to-earth way. If unbalanced, the red person will become furious and impatient with the orange person's irresponsibility and laziness, while the orange person
feels like an abused child and wishes that he or she were far away from the over-
bearing and hot-tempered red partner.

RELATIONSHIPS RED/YELLOW
This is not a very common relationship. The red person has
a stable and down-to-earth attitude to life, and the yellow
person has a philosophical and theoretical relationship to life.
Therefore, they will not always be able to understand each other. But if the red
person takes care of the practical things her/himself and lets the philosophical yellow partner control his/her own part of the relationship, then the two complement
each other well. Yellow people like to be taken care of in order to gain more free
time for philosophizing. Red people cherish the happy and optimistic life that

yellow people would create for them. Yet both people might develop more if they chose partners who understood them better. If unbalanced, it is hard for this couple to clear up misunderstandings. The red person with his/her physical and efficient solutions to all problems wants to fight back. The yellow person answers evasively and turn his/her back to the partner to find a new person that s/he can relate to better.

RELATIONSHIPS RED/GREEN
This is not an easy relationship, especially if the couple is unbalanced. When the red person becomes angry and explodes, the green person starts crying or becomes quiet and reserved. The green person wishes for peace, while the red person likes a good argument. The red person wants to receive vitality and passion from his/her partner while the green person wants sensitivity. When the green person talks about his/her emotions, the red person has difficulty understanding why s/he needs to talk about them. Green people are family oriented. Red people like to have the protector role in the family. Red people like to be spoiled, but above all they must be admired for their physical strength, powerful courage, and strong sex drive.

RELATIONSHIPS RED/BLUE
This can be a very dynamic couple. The blue person's ability to plan and organize combined with the red person's ability to realize plans is an outstanding combination. A red person sees the opportunity to realize plans as a wonderful challenge. The strong power that drives a red person fascinates a blue person. The blue person admires and values the red person's perseverance and will to go through with the hard challenges s/he takes on, while the red person admires the blue person's intelligence, mental strength, and ability to express her/himself. When balanced, they are each other's best support. The blue person needs the red person's fire and drive, and the red person needs the blue person's mental calmness. They are a very lively and outgoing couple with much respect for each other. But if they are unbalanced, they both have problems controlling their tempers. A red person can have a furious, uncontrollable temper. The blue person uses his/her sharp tongue to provoke the red person who will then quickly lose control over her/himself. The blue person does not hesitate to lay blame on the red person. Both people are strong willed and will want the last word in a fight.

Red Energy And Why You Are A Red Person

RELATIONSHIPS RED/INDIGO
These are two extremely different personalities–the physical
and grounded red person and the ethereal or esoteric indigo
person who has little or no relationship to his/her physical
body. The indigo person is so introverted and sensitive that s/he has
difficulty relating to the red person's extroverted and explosive energy. They are
only alike when it comes to their natural relationship to solitude and to working
alone. They will constantly misunderstand each other in discussions or conversations. They are miles apart when it comes to understanding problems or situations.

RELATIONSHIPS RED/VIOLET
This is an interesting combination. The violet person
has strong leadership qualities and has a great ability to
see into the future. The red person is inspired by this
and can help to realize the violet person's ideas. They are
both independent and strong-willed. The violet person's head and mind are
always in the clouds, while the red person has both feet on the ground. The violet person has deep feelings and is able to express them. Red people also have
deep feelings, but they cannot express themselves except in emotional
outbursts. When they are both in balance, they are able to work well together
as a team. The violet person is able to see all the good qualities of the red person. When unbalanced, the violet person orders the red person around. The
red person does not like this at all. In the same way, the red person thinks that
the violet person's ideas and thoughts are unrealistic, and thus s/he does not
respect the violet person. Because the red person has a realistic attitude, it can
be very difficult for the red person to relate to the violet person's way of foreseeing the future. The red person will often be skeptical about what the violet
person "sees."

Red Clothes
Wearing red clothing creates a vital, social, and independent image. Red is a sensual and passionate colour. The colour is best used for party clothes or underwear if
you are open to being approached or flirted with. In this connection, red shows
that you are not afraid of life or of the power and excitement this colour possesses.
At sporting events, red gives an impression of strength, power, and endurance. Do
not wear red if you are mad, frustrated, or over stimulated. Wear red when you
need to cheer yourself up. It also helps when you need the strong life qualities
which the red energies contain.

Red Interior Design

A room will seem smaller if you use a lot of red colour in it. In a room with a red ceiling, people may feel forced down and suffer claustrophobia. Personally, I think some red gives a feeling of excitement and stimulation to a room. On the other hand, red walls in a dining room is too forceful and can cause indigestion. In a red dining room you might eat too fast, because red increases blood circulation. Eating too fast can affect the digestive process. Since red affects sexual instincts, it might be a good idea to use red bedding once in a while. But usually red would be too disturbing for the bedroom, as it can cause restlessness and sleep problems.

Red Energy Drinks

Red drinks are stimulating and refreshing. Everybody would benefit from drinking a red drink every day. Red "sun-kissed water" can be easily made. Take a red glass and fill it with water. Place the glass in the sun for a few hours. You will end up with the cheapest and finest red energy you can treat your system to. This drink is a strong stimulant and will give you a physical energy boost. It can help alleviate temporary paralysis. It also will give you a sense of security and help you to develop your initiative. Lastly, it will stimulate your willpower and your courage. A real cordial!

Red Gemstones

The ruby is the main stone for red people. People who have red as their dominating colour could definitely benefit from wearing rubies. Rubies carry red energy and can strengthen the heart both psychologically and physically. The ruby's red energy works with the emotions and can help open up the heart so feelings run freely. This capacity strengthens a red person. A red person's judgment and actions will then take on a wider and more spiritual perspective.

Red Food

Food that has a high iron content usually contains red energy. For example, beets, spinach, and strawberries are red foods. Honey made from red flowers, such as red clover, will have a much stronger taste than honey made from other coloured flowers. Other red foods include meat, salmon, radishes, red cabbage, watercress, eggplants, cayenne pepper, tomatoes, cherries, watermelon, yams, red onions, red peppers, and other red–skinned or red–fleshed fruits and vegetables.

The Red Centre–Organs And Glands

Physically this chakra is linked to unconscious control mechanisms or our autonomic nervous system. The autonomic nervous system sustains our primary life instinct.

Affirmations For Red People

"Today I need help from your courage, your strength, and your love of life. I need your physical power, your willpower, your stamina, and your persistentness. I need red energy. I feel red. I am red."

Too Much Red Energy–Overactive

People with too much red energy become over absorbed in materialistic things and values–houses, cars, clothes, and food. They lose control of their natural relationship to sex. It shifts to crude pornography, perverse forms of sex, violence, and general abuse of their bodies.

Too Little Red Energy–Underactive

People with too little red energy lack down-to-earth common sense. They run away from responsibility and become insecure and cowardly. They believe that everyone is working against them and feel let down and abandoned.

Characteristics Of Red People

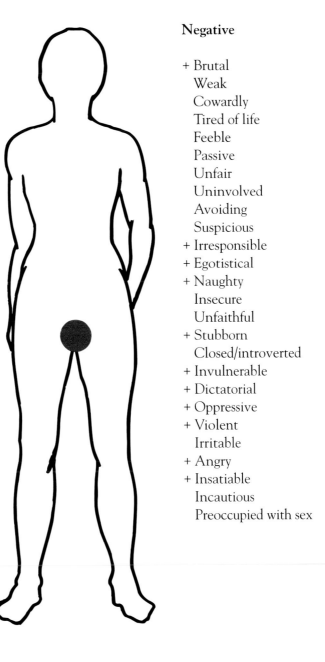

Positive

Sturdy
Strong
Brave
Happy with life
Vigorous
Energetic
Fair
Involved
Helpful
Sincere
+ Direct
Trusting
Responsible
Practical
Kind
Secure
Faithful
Firm/decisive
Open/extroverted
Honest
Warm/caring
Leader
Revolutionary
Calm
Great ability to love
Quick
Willing to take risks

Negative

+ Brutal
Weak
Cowardly
Tired of life
Feeble
Passive
Unfair
Uninvolved
Avoiding
Suspicious
+ Irresponsible
+ Egotistical
+ Naughty
Insecure
Unfaithful
+ Stubborn
Closed/introverted
+ Invulnerable
+ Dictatorial
+ Oppressive
+ Violent
Irritable
+ Angry
+ Insatiable
Incautious
Preoccupied with sex

Orange people ~
Orange sex ~ Orange health
~ Money and success for orange people ~
Occupations for orange people ~ Orange children
~ Orange parents ~ Orange relationships
~ Orange interior design ~ Orange energy
drinks ~ Orange gemstones ~ Orange food
~ The orange centre, organs and glands
~ Affirmations for orange people ~ Orange
energy, overactive and underactive
~ Orange positive and
negative

ORANGE ENERGY AND WHY YOU ARE AN ORANGE PERSON

Orange People

Orange people can behave more like a child than a grown-up. Many people think that orange people are childish, but being childish is not the same as being like a child. Orange people are happy and spontaneous. They have a wonderful ability to become awed with things. They are busy exploring the world in the same way children explore the world. It is refreshing to meet orange people, with their innocence and trust. They are friendly and open. They like people and people like them. They are social and love the outdoors. They love to organize parties, picnics, trips, and anything else that has to do with play, fun, and human relations. To other people, it seems as if orange people are socializing all the time. They are always surrounded by friends and family. But that is what they need–a secure relationship with family and children.

Orange people are lovers of life. With their happy and childlike behavior they help others to enjoy life and to not take themselves so seriously. The orange person reminds us of the child in ourselves. But even though the orange person appears worry-free and irresponsible, s/he still has strong feelings of personal responsibility for those who are weaker. Orange people always defend the weak. They often choose weak partners to make themselves feel that they are doing something important by helping them. Orange people have quick and sharp minds, but seldom have the time or the patience to study. They are always chasing new experiences, as they need constant stimulation and change. They love to move around, travel, and meet new people. Orange people are closest to themselves when they acknowledge and surrender to happiness. They learn about themselves through understanding their feelings and how their body reacts to feelings. It is very important that orange people plan and organize their lives so that they are personally satisfied. When they are in balance, they set a good example for others to follow. Besides being smart, they are also very creative. But they are more practical than intellectual. A theory-based education is not appropriate for an orange person. An education in which theory and practice alternate is best. They are not intellectuals and they need to use tricks to help them maintain their concentration when studying. For example, they could play tapes on a headphone while jogging to help them learn difficult subject matter. They love to brag, and they tend to exaggerate.

Orange people also tend to eat too much or too little. They are constantly on diets. They usually try to control their weight with aerobic exercise, but aerobic exercise is not suitable for them. Orange people are naturally predisposed to knee, elbow, and shoulder injuries. Because aerobic exercise stresses the skeleton, joints, and vertebrae, orange people should rely on other exercises such as walking, swimming, cycling, and dancing. Tai-chi, yoga, and other active forms of meditation are also very good for orange people's bodies and souls. These forms of exercise calm the body and mind to help new ideas flow freely. In this way the body and soul come into balance. But it is not easy for orange people to get rid of their restlessness because they often over stimulate their bio-chemical system. For example, if orange people wake up in the morning with a feeling of restlessness or indisposition, they will start the day by drinking coffee, eating white sugar, and smoking a cigarette and, in the worst-case scenario, drinking alcohol or taking drugs to calm their feelings.

It is very easy for orange people to become addicted to drugs and alcohol. They want to feel good, and this deep hunger for well-being often takes them in the wrong direction. It is incredibly important for orange people to find a balance and a sense of physical well-being. There are a lot of negative temptations for orange people, such as coffee, chocolate, soft drinks, white sugar, cigarettes, wine, beer, alcohol, prescription drugs, and narcotics.

Sex can be a positive stimulant for orange people. Sex releases tensions and leaves a feeling of well-being. When having an orgasm, an orange person can touch a part of their inner self. Orange people's senses are connected to physical feelings. Their bio-chemical system is constantly sending them messages on how they think and feel. Although orange people seem free, independent, happy and confident, they have an inner insecure side that they rarely show. It is as if orange people flee from an inner voice that they do not want to listen to. Orange people have a hard time with self-discovery and exploring aspects of themselves. This is one of the reasons why orange people often run away from relationships that become too demanding and complicated. They choose the easy way out. You might say they were shallow if you did not know that underneath this indifferent attitude is a fear of revealing a confusing picture of themselves. "Don't worry," "be happy," and "everything will be all right" are the mottoes of orange people.

Orange Sex

Orange people are sex-oriented. They like the love game and have a lot of fun with sex. They like refined sex stories and like going to sex shops to buy special presents for their friends. Sex is fun for them. However, they are very loyal and sensitive. They can be extremely attentive to their partners. They are proud to be monogamous. They flirt a lot when out for the evening, but they are not serious and they will always withdraw if the person they are flirting with should expect more.

Orange Health

The positive and worry-free orange people are amongst the most refreshing and health-oriented people on earth. They are natural-born healers and usually live long lives. Their natural ability to let the universal energy flow through their bodies keeps them healthy.

Orange people have a tremendous sense of smell. They like to smell food before eating it. If they smell something they do not like, they will avoid where the smell is coming from. They are very obsessive about body odour.

Their physical weak spots are the back and the knees. When orange people are not in balance, these two spots are very vulnerable. They easily catch colds, especially when they are feeling down. Orange people have so much energy, though, that they can readily heal themselves. When an orange person becomes ill, it is a sure sign that the person is not in balance. Fear is an orange person's worst enemy.

The orange colour energy can affect our interests and activities. Orange increases the intake of oxygen and stimulates the lungs. Orange is good when you are doing breathing exercises. It can help to heal lung diseases. It removes gas from the digestive tract and is an effective cure for hiccups and menstrual cramps.

Health Tips For Orange People

How we eat tells us a lot about how we react to things and events in our life, especially regarding sex. How do we relate to our food? Do we play with our food or do we gulp it down? Anorexia and bulimia are connected to this issue as well. Orange people need to use their yellow energy to help them control their sex life and eating disorders. They need the green energy to love themselves and the indigo and violet to get more spiritual energy.

Money And Success For Orange People

It does not take much money for an orange person to be happy. Money is everything or nothing. They would prefer it if someone could look after them financially. They do not mind working, but they do not like to work too hard for their money. They seldom know how they have spent the money they earned. They are irresponsible with money and not financially stable. Orange people have to work very hard to save money. They judge their success on their popularity and on how much fun and freedom they have had.

Occupations For Orange People

Orange people make great artists, musicians, massage therapists, diplomats, social workers, and politicians. They are born healers. They also make good health consultants, dietitians, veterinarians, athletes, flight attendants, tour guides, receptionists, restaurant managers, bartenders, and doctors.

Orange Children

Orange children are very curious and active. They have difficulty sitting still. At school, teachers should let these children do creative work with their hands–drawing, knitting, or modeling–when they are studying theoretical subjects. They love to learn, but to just sit there and listen for long periods of time is not appropriate for their learning style. They become restless and cannot concentrate. They are often the class clown, as they like to make others happy. It is not advisable for parents or teachers to try to make these children sit tight and listen. Orange children always make playing their first priority. They want to have fun, make things up, and be creative. When orange children feel that they are liked and accepted for who they are, their self-worth is in balance and they are very easy to work with. They do not like to hurt anybody's feelings. They easily pick up moods between parents and can react strongly when parents fight. They would like their parents to become friends again right away. If this does not happen, they think that it was their fault and become very depressed and reserved.

Just like red children, orange children need to get rid of their frustrations. If angry, they may hit or break something. Parents should teach their children how to burn off energy in positive ways. Running, cycling, and playing active games are good ideas. Punishment and discipline does not help when orange children have too much energy. Orange children are the ones who react best to physical punishment. But if physical punishment is used too much, the children will lose their self-respect and self-esteem. Parents often use this form of power, when they see how readily orange children react to physical punishment.

Orange Energy And Why You Are An Orange Person

Orange Parents

Orange parents make good playmates for their children, because they are childlike themselves. A woman who is married to an orange man often feels that she has an extra child.

Orange parents love to play with children, but they do not necessarily like the job of raising children. They do not particularly like the responsibility of teaching children the practical things of life. They like to be friends with their children.

Orange parents can set a bad example for their children if they lack energy. They can become lazy and avoid responsibility. When orange parents are frustrated and troubled they frequently express this in a physical way, by hitting and breaking things or by running away from their problems. It can be very difficult for children if alcohol and drugs enter the picture.

Orange Relationships

Orange people are not easy to live with if you try to control them. Orange people often have an idealistic view of how a relationship should be. They want to have a partner they can laugh with and have a good time with. They need to have a partner who can take care of them (but not like a mother), and still give them the freedom they need. Despite their social nature, they need time to themselves.

Orange people love the excitement of flirting, but they run from any type of commitment. They are scared of the responsibility and obligations a relationship requires. They avoid responsibility and obligation by desiring or falling in love with someone they can't have. In this way they feel secure in their own unhappy situation. A paradox. But if an orange person is in balance, in love, and in a stable relationship, he or she is loving, kind, protective, and faithful. They will do everything to make the chosen one happy.

When out of balance, orange people feel trapped. Duties and responsibilities make them feel depressed and unhappy. Unbalanced orange people often initiate fights and provoke their partners. When orange people lack energy, they often take drugs, alcohol, tranquilizers, etc., to comfort themselves. This can really be harmful to an orange person. Orange people need happiness in their lives and lots of encouragement. They should be allowed to express the childlike side of themselves.

Orange Energy And Why You Are An Orange Person

RELATIONSHIPS ORANGE/ORANGE

Two orange people are good for each other. They will understand each other's need for freedom and solitude. They both have a strong need to perform physical activities and to be with people. When in balance, they live a life full of laughter and happiness. They will enjoy earthly pleasures together, give each other energy, and complement each other. When unbalanced, orange people can become emotionally unstable and avoid coming to terms with their unbalanced selves. They easily get into financial trouble and have problems clearing the situation up. If one partner gets involved with drugs or alcohol, the other partner can be dragged in too. Orange people lack self-discipline, and one will pull the other down.

RELATIONSHIPS ORANGE/RED

In this relationship, the two people are strong physically, but that is where the similarities end. The red person uses willpower energy, while the orange person uses emotional energy. The sensitive and emotional orange person is easily dominated by the strong red person. The red person, on the other hand, can provide stability in the orange person's life. Since an orange person can often be childlike and indecisive, the red person can take on a protective and caring role. They both like physical work and are constantly rearranging their furniture. They both also like to work outside and around the house. Frequently they have the same kind of hobbies or occupations. The red person is the responsible one in the relationship, and the orange person is the one who brings laughter and happiness into the life of the hard-working red person. If in balance, the two people enjoy life together in a down-to-earth way. If unbalanced, the red person will become furious and impatient with the orange person's irresponsibility and laziness, while the orange person feels like an abused child and wishes that he or she were far away from the overbearing and hot-tempered red partner.

RELATIONSHIPS ORANGE/YELLOW

This is a very exciting relationship. The yellow person feels very attracted to the happy and creative orange person. The two always have something to discuss, as the orange person usually has lots of interests and likes to be well-informed about everything. They learn a great deal from each other. The orange person can be emotionally domineering and protective of the yellow person. The yellow person should allow the orange person to create the type of environment that s/he is comfortable in. The intelligent and logical yellow person quickly sees through the superficial orange person. But s/he will have great patience and confidence in the orange person's values. The yellow person will have to take charge of their finances, unless they wish to live like Bohemians. If unbalanced, the orange person runs one way and the yellow person the other way. Neither of them wishes to face conflicts or problems. They both run from any financial responsibility.

RELATIONSHIPS ORANGE/GREEN

Relationships between an orange person and a green person are very common. These two personalities are attracted to each other. The protective and loving green person is very attracted to the childlike orange person. The orange person gets all the love s/he needs from the protective and caring green person. The green person will takes care of the finances as well.

When a green person is in love, s/he wants to be near his or her partner all the time. This does not always suit the orange person, as s/he needs time alone. The green person feels hurt and takes it personally when the orange person wants to be by her/himself. An orange person does not like to hurt anybody and will often leave unnoticed just to avoid confrontation. An orange person feels guilty easily, and a green person knows how to use this. When in balance, they are a very friendly couple. They are both sensitive and like to help people. They are both ruled by their emotions and need to be balanced in order to give each other their best. When in balance, the green person can laugh at the orange person's ideas and stories and even accept the orange person's need to give gifts now and then. In return, the orange person has to understand the green person's crying spells and need for companionship. The orange person must learn not to run each time something happens that s/he has to take a stand on. The green person needs to feel loved for what s/he is. The green person must get better at helping the orange person gain self-confidence and independence. The green person is on earth to give love and the orange person to give happiness and to heal. They can be a wonderful couple, especially if they can work well together.

RELATIONSHIPS ORANGE/BLUE

This can be a challenging relationship. They will learn a tremendous amount from each other, because they do not share the same standards or goals. The blue person is good at realizing ideas and plans and will be inspired by the

vital and creative orange person. The blue person is a great manager while the orange person is an artist. As long as this couple is in balance, they compliment each other's talents. The couple then has the potential of going far in life together. The blue person needs admiration and respect from other people. And this is the best thing the orange person can give his/her partner. Since a blue person teaches by example, an orange person learns easily from her or him. The orange person hates to be told what to do.

If unbalanced, the orange person will feel oppressed by a blue partner. The orange person then works her/himself up and provokes the blue partner. In response, an unbalanced blue person will verbally abuse the orange person back. Verbal abuse is something an orange person cannot defend her/himself against. The orange person has to understand that a blue person lives differently. Blue people often feel frustrated and irritated by their own behavior. They are perfectionists and have a hard time living up to their own standards. The orange person can help the blue person to take life a little less seriously and teach the blue person to laugh at herself or himself. Admiration and respect is the best gift a blue person can receive from an orange person.

RELATIONSHIPS ORANGE/INDIGO

Orange and indigo people make good friends. The orange person's attitude towards play and happiness fascinates the indigo person, just as the indigo person's attitude to the other world attracts the orange person. They both are dominated by emotional energies and are fascinated by people and human relations. They both wish to be liked by other people. They are both stubborn and like to do their own thing. While the indigo person strives for a soul-to-soul relationship, the orange person seeks a carefree, no-obligation relationship. The orange person lives in the here and now and is not looking for a soul mate. If balanced, they will gain a lot from each other. They can teach each other about life as seen from two different perspectives–the indigo person with his/her spiritual focus and the orange person's focus on earthly pleasures. If unbalanced, it is likely that they will not be able to help each other much. The indigo person will lose confidence in the irresponsible orange person, and the orange person will accuse the indigo person of being flaky and living in a dreamland. An unbalanced indigo person will constantly have identity crises. Indigo people lose their balance quickly. An unbalanced orange person will not be able to provide the support the indigo person needs. The orange person will have no self-confidence and will be full of fear. The indigo person and orange person are then a couple in which the blind try to lead the blind.

RELATIONSHIPS ORANGE/VIOLET

Orange and violet people can have a lot of fun together. They are both creative and inspire each other. The
violet person understands and respects the orange per-
son's need for happiness, play, and freedom. They are both
happy when they socialize. They both like unconventional and improvised
forms of parties. They both have enormous energy resources and enjoy sex. Usually, the violet person is the leader in the relationship as s/he has drive and an
intuitive understanding of the purpose and meaning of life. When in balance,
these two have a lot of common interests—music, entertainment, sex, travel,
physical exercise, and people. They experience life together and complement
each other fully. To others, they seem like a very harmonious and dynamic couple. If unbalanced, the orange person seems lazy, preoccupied, and irresponsible.
The violet person will become frustrated and disappointed with an orange partner who is unfaithful, irresponsible with money, and comforts her/himself
through substance abuse. The violet person, on the other hand, can become so
arrogant and act so superior that the orange person is intimidated and loses
his/her self-confidence.

Orange Interior Design

Orange has inspirational qualities. It gives off warmth and an atmosphere of well-
being. Kitchens, playrooms, and recreational rooms benefit from orange in any
shade. Orange is also great for dining rooms and restaurants. It is an ideal colour
for delis and bakeries. Children like this colour a lot.

Orange Energy Drinks

Orange drinks are perfect for bronchitis and asthma. Orange energy strengthens
the lungs and helps increase oxygen intake.

Orange Gemstones

The carnelian is the main stone for orange people. The orange energy of the carnelian balances positive and negative flows. It is important for orange people to
maintain a balance. This balancing act is what orange people have to learn in
their lives.

Orange Food

If you need orange energy, the best kind of food is fruit–oranges, papayas, peaches, melons, mangos, and clementines. Carrots and orange peppers are extremely good too.

The Orange Centre–Organs And Glands

The orange chakra is connected to the splenic nervous centre, which influences the working of the spleen. The spleen functions as a blood cleanser. It also breaks down the energy in food. The spleen centre stimulates the urge for a social commitment.

Affirmations For Orange People

"Today I need help from your happiness in the present, your warmth, your spontaneity, your freedom from care, and your lack of restraint. I need orange energy. I feel orange. I am orange."

Too Much Orange Energy–Overactive

Overactive orange energy expresses itself like a demanding child that has never grown up. Overactive orange energy does only what it wants to do. Overactive orange energy can lead to sex addiction. Luxurious food and drinks, and a demanding social life will drain the orange person of energy. Too much or too little orange energy leads to a drug dependency or other addictive behavior.

Too Little Orange Energy–Underactive

The orange energy turns inwards, and the resulting insecurity and lack of faith in oneself leads to dishonesty and irresponsible behavior towards one's job. Depression occurs if there is no happiness or contact with one's inner child.

The Characteristics Of Orange People

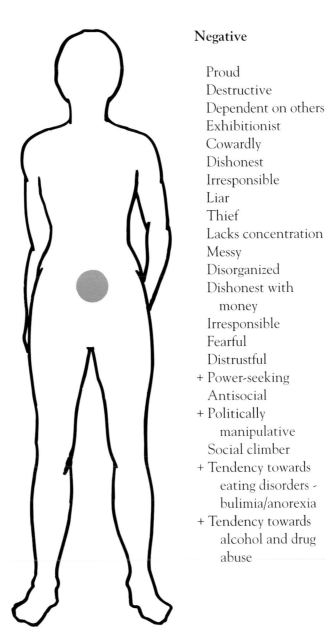

Positive

Happy
Enthusiastic
Independent
Social
Loves food
Energetic
Athletic
Health-oriented
Confident
Constructive
Creative
Outgoing
Funny
Talkative
Likes children
Likes people
Likes to go out
Spreads happiness
Entertaining
Spontaneous
Humanistic
Warm
Optimistic
Ambitious
Competitive
Playful
Loving
+ Generous
Great ability to heal
Good therapist

Negative

Proud
Destructive
Dependent on others
Exhibitionist
Cowardly
Dishonest
Irresponsible
Liar
Thief
Lacks concentration
Messy
Disorganized
Dishonest with
   money
Irresponsible
Fearful
Distrustful
+ Power-seeking
Antisocial
+ Politically
   manipulative
Social climber
+ Tendency towards
   eating disorders -
   bulimia/anorexia
+ Tendency towards
   alcohol and drug
   abuse

Yellow people ~
Yellow sex ~ Yellow health
~ Money and success for yellow people
~ Occupations for yellow people ~ Yellow
children ~ Yellow parents ~ Yellow relationships
~ Yellow interior design ~ Yellow energy
drinks ~ Yellow gemstones ~ Yellow food ~
The yellow centre, organs and glands ~
Affirmations for yellow people ~ Yellow
energy, overactive and underactive
~ Yellow positive and
negative

YELLOW ENERGY AND
WHY YOU ARE A YELLOW PERSON

Yellow People

Yellow people are hungry for knowledge. Because of this, they are open and susceptible to new facts and impressions. Yellow people are explorers and researchers. They are sensitive, pleasant, well-mannered, polite, and kind. They are good listeners. They are often collectors of philosophies, knowledge, and ideas, but they also collect other things such as books, stamps, beer caps, or empty milk cartons.

Many yellow people want to cut themselves off from everybody else. They can isolate themselves as bookworms, librarians, hermits, ascetics, and monks. They read and study tremendously. This often affects their eyes, which is why so many yellow people wear glasses. Yellow people are strong-willed. Many yellow people have great control over their willpower and emotions. The yellow energy centre controls willpower and feelings.

When in balance, yellow people are like the sun itself–warm, open, and positive towards everything. They can laugh, cry, and have a good natural relationship with their bodies. But when in a negative state, they tend to chain-in their emotions. Yellow people can then seem to be cool, haughty, and judgmental. In jobs involving people, especially in bureaucratic departments, yellow people can be very authoritarian. Power follows in the wake of knowledge and it is easy to misuse it.

Yellow people are very conservative about food, clothes, and shelter. They tend to spend their time at the intellectual level. They like debating issues, throwing ideas around, and organizing systems. Their biggest asset is their ability to think logically. They do not usually rely on their intuition or feelings. The only thing that counts for yellow people is facts and written words. When out of balance, it is easy for them to become skeptical and suspicious. Yellow people feel better in an abstract world. They have no ideals or ideas about changing the world. When balanced, they will have many friends with whom they socialize. When unbalanced, they tend to divide friends into groups. One group of friends will know nothing about the other group. Negative energies can bring out obsessive collecting, greed and avarice in yellow people. Here avarice has to be underlined, because yellow people are usually such careful people with minimal need for material things.

Yellow Sex

Yellow people have to feel comfortable with their partners. They are seldom passionate. They live in their heads and therefore, in a way, sex takes place in their minds. They would feel very vulnerable if they displayed too much emotion to another human being. Sex is not a top priority for yellow people, but they like to have sex with a safe partner.

Yellow Health

A yellow person's illness pattern is often so changing that it is difficult to diagnose. They frequently have many health concerns, but most of them are not serious. A lot of their illnesses have a psychosomatic cause. Illness usually occurs when they are frustrated. Yellow people understand better than blue people that they need to exercise and have a healthy diet.

Health Tips For Yellow People

Yellow people often suppress their feelings of depression. They do not know how to handle depression. Bloodshot eyes can be a sign that the yellow fire energy is being blocked. If you bite your tongue and hold everything in, anger will create problems in the digestive tract. You can get an ulcer, spleen and liver problems, headaches, and pressure behind the eyes from gas build-up in the digestive tract. Mental constipation is also a possibility. Negative thoughts and holding onto old ways of thinking can create rigid attitudes.

Money And Success For Yellow People

Security and stability are important factors for yellow people. Money as such is not the most important thing, but they need to know that they have enough to live on. They usually have long-term investments and are well-informed about their pensions and retirement plans. They do not fritter away their money but spend it practically and reasonably. Yellow people measure their success by the amount of schooling they have had and by what they have learned. They like the feeling of having planned for their future, both in work and in their private affairs. They need to feel that they have definite boundaries in their lives.

Occupations For Yellow People

Yellow people need jobs that allow them to use their friendly, optimistic, curious, bright, and insightful minds. This keeps them satisfied and healthy. Yellow people are often drawn to intellectually challenging work. They make good architects, bookkeepers, market analysts, computer analysts, mathematicians, researchers, data processors, professors, librarians, court reporters, office clerks, engineers, teachers, psychologists, city planners, and technical writers.

Yellow Children

Yellow children are happy, impulsive, and intelligent. They learn fast and remember well. They have a huge thirst for knowledge and can almost always be found in the children's section of a library. They have many friends and like to be in a group. They are kind and friendly to be around. They often take part in exchange programs with other countries, as they are good at learning languages. When they lack energy, yellow children often fall prey to flattery. They might become sly and ingratiate themselves with parents and teachers. When they have too much energy they will become arrogant and think they are intellectually superior. They look down on all those who are not as smart as they are.

Yellow Parents

Yellow parents are very occupied with learning. They look forward to becoming parents, because then they will learn even more. They will learn about childcare, child psychology, and nutrition for children. They are frequently more occupied with what goes on around the child rather than with the child. They will be interested in their children's schooling and in the right toys and games. They like to discuss things with their children, and they believe that children should have opinions of their own. They respect their children and let them live their own lives.

Yellow Relationships

When balanced, yellow people are mentally creative. They have incredible self-respect. They let everyone be who they want to be and live their lives the way they want to. They are optimistic and happy, and prefer to live life in a positive way. They are strong-willed and like to live independent lives. They like to be around fun people who interest them. They like to learn about people, and often they marry several times. They deal with divorce in a civilized and friendly way. They do not wish to hurt their partners, since they are typically very kind. They are often friends with ex-partners for the rest of their lives. When unbalanced, yellow people will tend to isolate themselves. They become suspicious, skeptical, and pessimistic towards everything and everybody. Furthermore, they become cunning, cowardly, and withdrawn. They want to close all doors leading to feelings and sympathy.

Yellow Energy And Why You Are A Yellow Person

RELATIONSHIPS YELLOW/YELLOW

This is a happy couple. They both will have many interests.
They will want to be each other's best friend and support.
They will like to discuss things together and with others. They
are well-educated and interested in life. Whether they are intellectual Bohemians or university graduates, they enjoy the life around them. They do
not have big materialistic goals, but they know how to manage money and are seldom in need. When balanced, they have incredible intellectual strength and give
each other great inspiration and happiness. When unbalanced, they become pessimistic and skeptical of their partners and of new things. Yellow people are dependent on the love they receive from the people who are closest to them and they do
not thrive if negative thinking surrounds them.

RELATIONSHIPS YELLOW/RED

This is not a very common relationship. The red person
has a stable and down-to-earth attitude to life, and the yellow person has a philosophical and theoretical relationship
to life. Therefore, they will not always be able to understand each
other. But if the red person takes care of the practical things her/himself and lets
the philosophical yellow partner control his/her own part of the relationship, then
the two complement each other well. Yellow people like to be taken care of in
order to gain more free time for philosophizing. Red people cherish the happy and
optimistic life that yellow people would create for them. Yet both people might
develop more if they chose partners who understood them better. If unbalanced, it
is hard for this couple to clear up misunderstandings. The red person with his/her
physical and efficient solutions to all problems wants to fight back. The yellow person answers evasively and turn his/her back to the partner to find a new person
that s/he can relate to better.

RELATIONSHIPS YELLOW/ORANGE

This is a very exciting relationship. The yellow person
feels very attracted to the happy and creative orange person. The two always have something to discuss, as the
orange person usually has lots of interests and likes to be well-
informed about everything. They learn a great deal from each other. The orange
person can be emotionally domineering and protective of the yellow person. The
yellow person should allow the orange person to create the type of environment
that s/he is comfortable in. The intelligent and logical yellow person quickly sees
through the superficial orange person. But s/he will have great patience and confidence in the orange person's values. The yellow person will have to take charge of

their finances, unless they wish to live like Bohemians. If unbalanced, the orange person runs one way and the yellow person the other way. Neither of them wishes to face conflicts or problems. They both run from any financial responsibility.

RELATIONSHIPS YELLOW/GREEN

A yellow person will get along easily with a green person. They will grow in all ways together. The green person's loving and sacrificing ways will be a good support to the impractical and philosophical yellow person. The green person will admire his/her partner's intelligence, good sense of humor, and optimistic view of life. The yellow person will feel comfortable surrounded by the green person's care. Both will be happy with life as it is. When unbalanced, the yellow person becomes selfish and pessimistic. S/he will blame the green person for not being intellectual enough. The green person will seem too simple-minded and kind for the shrewd and skeptical yellow person. The green person will feel emotionally neglected and will complain about not being understood or valued enough.

RELATIONSHIPS YELLOW/BLUE

Again this is a good relationship, especially at the intellectual level. The yellow person with his/her knowledge, intellectual pursuits, sense of humor, and kindness stimulates and interests the blue person. The blue person will inspire the yellow person with his/her wisdom and ability to reach goals. This relationship enables both partners to grow and to develop new ideas in areas such as research, teaching methods, politics, and inventions. Anything will be possible in this relationship. When unbalanced, they lose faith in each other and become pessimistic and negative. The blue person becomes sarcastic and says hurtful things. The yellow person acts in cowardly way, avoiding any confrontation.

RELATIONSHIPS YELLOW/ INDIGO

This couple can do well together if they are both balanced. They are both naturally helpful. They both seek the truth–the yellow person through philosophy and theories, and the indigo person through an inner belief system–yet, each respects the other's differences. Financially they are comfortable, but their cheque books never balance. An indigo person feels happy with a positive yellow person, mostly because the yellow person is intelligent and well informed about things. The yellow person also tolerates people and is not judgmental. When unbalanced, they both withdraw into themselves. The indigo person lives in his/her inner world. The yellow person turns his/her skepticism and pessimism against the world and retreats.

Yellow Energy And Why You Are A Yellow Person

RELATIONSHIPS YELLOW/VIOLET

This is a good connection. The yellow person is stimulated by the creative and intelligent violet person and inspired by the violet person's spiritual orientation. The violet person is inspired by the yellow person's theoretical  and philosophical orientation. The violet person can also be very artistic. In this case, the yellow person supports the violet partner with optimism and confidence in the violet person's new ideas and ideals. When unbalanced, the violet person's spiritual inspiration can easily turn to the occult and black magic. This is something the yellow person has difficulty understanding. If the yellow person lacks energy, s/he becomes pessimistic and negative and does not make an effort to solve shared problems.

Yellow Interior Design

Yellow is good for study areas. On the other hand, it is not recommended as a bedroom colour or for places where people wish to relax. It is a stimulating colour and thus would be great for a bookstore. All shades of yellow can be used in living rooms.

Yellow Energy Drinks

Diabetics and people who suffer from digestive problems would benefit from yellow energy drinks. A glass every morning would be a very good idea.

Yellow Gemstones

The main stone for yellow people is the citrine. Citrine acts like a magnet for the yellow energy ray. It is not a strong stone, but it brings a lot of light and sound to the wearer. This stone is good for cleaning the chakras, especially if the chakras are closed. Vibrations from the stone will slowly open the chakras. It is important to let the citrine lie in the sun for several hours to cleanse it.

Yellow Food

There is yellow energy in yellow fruits and vegetables such as lemons, grapefruits, pineapples, bananas, papayas, peaches, turnips, cabbages, apricots, carrots, yellow peppers, corn, and yellow squash. Yellow energy is also present in egg yolks, olive oil, and butter.

The Yellow Centre–Organs And Glands

The yellow centre is connected to the solar plexus. The solar plexus affects the adrenal glands, which produce the powerful nerve stimulant adrenaline. The solar plexus represents the ability to freely express self-confidence and self-interest.

Affirmations For Yellow People

"I need help today from your desire to gain knowledge. I need your curiosity, and your clear, logical energy. I need to feel the sun shine on me and give me peace. I need the yellow energy. I feel yellow. I am yellow."

Too Much Yellow Energy–Overactive

In this situation the solar plexus works overtime, and the person becomes over-bearing, domineering, and judgmental. People in this condition want things their way, no matter what. The negative energy draws them into manipulative ways.

Too Little Yellow Energy–Underactive

In this situation, skepticism and over-criticism are pronounced. No emotions will be let in or out. The person becomes controlling. Rules and regulations are unquestioningly followed. The person thinks it is dangerous to have uncensored free thinking.

Characteristics Of Yellow People

Positive

Good sense of humor
Many interests
Optimistic
Trusting
Clear thinking
Far-sighted
Thirsty for knowledge
Knowledgeable
Thoughtful
Fun
Simple
Straightforward
Kind
Not snobbish
+ Thrifty
Conscientious
Likes to spread happiness
Likes to have many friends
Team player
Logical
Analytical
Flexible
Methodical
Punctual

Negative

+ Likes flattery
+ Exaggerates
Pessimistic
+ Sly
+ Calculating
Cowardly
Skeptical
Secretive
Elusive
Arrogant
+ Intolerant
+ Greedy
Absent-minded
+Egocentric
Suspicious
+ Critical
Schizophrenic
Self-centred
Judgmental
+ Verbally abusive
+ Unfeeling

Green people ~
Green sex ~ Green health ~
Money and success for green people ~
Occupations for green people ~ Green
children ~ Green parents ~ Green relationships
~ Green interior design ~ Green energy drinks
~ Green gemstones ~ Green food ~ The green
centre, organs and glands ~ Affirmations for
green people ~ Green energy, overactive
and underactive ~ Green positive
and negative

GREEN ENERGY AND WHY YOU ARE A GREEN PERSON

Green People

Green people like other people and people like them. They always put aside their own needs to help others. This is a good quality that they can teach others. Green people have a need to be loved and to feel that someone loves them. Green energy is sensitive and full of emotions. Green people are like small sweet bear cubs, who need to be played with and cared for. When in love, they love with all their heart.

Green people are the givers and helpers in our society. They are always there to help family, friends, and co-workers. Charity organizations and bazaars would not exist without green people. They often have several close friends. Green people like to have meaningful friendships. They do their best to gain their friends' trust and faith and often give their friends advice and help. They love flattery and praise. All in all, they love to feel important to other people.

Green people have quite a bit of natural emotional intuition. Green people think holistically, like the other three emotional colours. They can easily see the essence of a problem, but frequently they cannot express what it is they see. They often let their feelings show through tears or laughter. Their tendency to show their feeling can embarrass them, but it is a good quality. If they held in their feelings they would become frustrated and blocked. Green people are deeply touched by many things–a beautiful sunset, church music, being with someone they love. When unbalanced, they help more than necessary and their helpfulness becomes over-bearing. If green people get hurt, they can become totally furious. Often it is very hard for them to show their true selves. They can listen to other people's complaints, but they have difficulty being natural about their own problems.

Green Sex

Green people express love in the form of devotion to their partners. Often their expectations of what a sexual relationship should be based on do not include animal instinct or strong passion. Romance should bloom first, and when love flows the sexual act will naturally follow. Green people carry deep feelings, and they often feel like crying or saying many things to the partner during sex. They seldom get any particular satisfaction out of their sexual relationships, because to them sex can be something impure. They have difficulty forming good relationships, as they have to trust their partner one hundred percent and feel that it is true love.

Green Health

The weak side of green people is their nervousness about their own health. They often worry themselves into ulcers and intestinal problems. The stomach and intestines are their weak spots. It is therefore really important for green people to stay balanced if they have any physical symptoms of illnesses. Green people should walk a lot and should learn how to breathe properly and how to meditate. They can become better balanced if they learn to give themselves just as much love and care as they give others. Green women often have problems with their breasts, with their ovaries, and with vaginal infections because they often feel guilty, ashamed, and inadequate when it come to sex. Green people prefer team sports such as volleyball, bowling, riding, swimming, and dancing. Most of all they like to walk and to participate in marches. Green women gain weight easily, especially after childbirth. They often have large and fairly round bodies. Green women who do not feel loved or who do not love themselves will often put on a few pounds around the hips to protect their sexual feelings and this extra weight tends to stay. The beauty of mature green people lies in their ability to take care of others and to give others a feeling of well-being.

A Heart Exercise:

So many things in this world make us react with sorrow. Do this exercise when your grief causes your heart area to hurt or if you are depressed and totally down—when you feel that your heart is crushed. Here is one thing you can do before you actually get heart disease. Open up your heart and cry if you can. Let the tears run freely. Know that someone out there hears your prayers.

Base your prayers on any religion you want to. Let the words formulate from your throat chakra. It is very important get rid of all your negative feelings before the heart chakra becomes blocked. It might be helpful to say these Tibetan holy words, which have helped hundreds and thousands of people to clean their souls: OM - ALT - HUM - VAJRA - GURU - PASMA - SIDDI - HUM. Or say the Lord's Prayer. Use anything you can think of to help link your voice and prayers to higher spiritual energies.

Money And Success For Green People

Green people are good givers, but they are not good at receiving. They often feel that the work they do has to come from the heart and not from a desire for money. Because money does not have top priority, they often feel that they do not have enough money, especially if they have families. They also frequently choose careers that do not pay well. This is a major complaint of theirs. Green people should learn that growth, whether spiritual or materialistic, is an energy in itself and not a sin. Green people base their success on how many people they have been able to help, how many friends they have, and the length of their marriages. They like to help people and often choose jobs in which they can do this.

Occupations For Green People

Green people make good teachers, nurses, counselors, childcare workers, secretaries, clergy assistants, nuns, parents, social workers, gardeners, florists, veterinarians, forest rangers, real estate agents, bankers, and healers.

Green Children

Green children are very sensitive and kind. Usually they play inside, where they can sit quietly and comb a doll's hair or play with building blocks. Green children like to take care of others and to defend the weak. They become sad if they feel that someone is lonely, as they believe that everyone should have someone they love. Green children have many friends. When green children lack energy, they feel lonely and uncared for and this can lead to low self-esteem and low self-respect.

Green Parents

Green parents are protective and loving. They are so emotionally tied to their children that they would like to spare them from all unpleasant experiences. This can make the children very unsure of themselves. The children think the parents do not have faith in their abilities. Children of green parents often feel guilty when they move away from home. Green parents have to learn not to make their children dependent on them. There are so many other people they can help. The world is full of people who need help.

Green Relationships

Green people wish, more than anything else, to have warm relationships. Good, loving relationships stimulate green people and make them feel that life is worth living. Loneliness can be depressing for green people. A good relationship is so important to green people that they will do anything–change their hairdo, clothes, lifestyle, and attitude–to please their partner and to become the person they think their partner wants. Green people have so much love and care to give that they often stifle their partner's colour energy. They would like to be around their loved ones all the time. They often feel slighted or unloved if the partner withdraws to be alone for a little while. If they lack energy, green people may choose wrong partners, often someone they can save and take care of, or someone who wants to physically or psychologically hurt them. They cannot cope with the feelings of guilt during divorce, so they ignore marital problems and stay in unhappy marriages longer than they should. They think that if they are patient and loving, everything will work out. If the relationship is definitely over, they throw themselves into a new relationship with whoever comes first.

RELATIONSHIPS GREEN/GREEN

A green/green relationship is similar to a relationship between identical twins. The two people think and feel the same way. They cry over the same sensitive parts at the theatre or in real life situations. They understand each other's need to let their emotions run free. Green people are loyal and have a high ethical regard for friendships and relationships so it takes a lot to make them wish their partners harm. If they separate, they stay friends. When in balance, they give each other all the love they need. They seem like an extremely harmonious couple to the outside world. Without energy and balance, green people can be very moody. They take everything personally. One sharp remark and green people feel hurt and withdraw into themselves. If unbalanced, green people often take a the martyr role or use guilt to their advantage.

RELATIONSHIPS GREEN/RED

This is not an easy relationship, especially if the couple is unbalanced. When the red person becomes angry and explodes, the green person starts crying or becomes quiet and reserved. The green person wishes for peace, while the red person likes a good argument. The red person wants to receive vitality and passion from his/her partner while the green person wants sensitivity. When the green person talks about his/her emotions, the red person has difficulty understanding why s/he needs to talk about them. Green people are family oriented. Red people like to have the protector role in the family. Red people like to be spoiled, but above all they must be admired for their physical strength, powerful courage, and strong sex drive.

Green Energy And Why You Are A Green Person

RELATIONSHIPS GREEN/ORANGE

Relationships between an orange person and a green person are very common. These two personalities are attracted to each other. The protective and loving green person is very attracted to the childlike orange person. The orange person gets all the love s/he needs from the protective and caring green person. The green person will take care of the finances as well.

When a green person is in love, s/he wants to be near his or her partner all the time. This does not always suit the orange person, as s/he needs time alone. The green person feels hurt and takes it personally when the orange person wants to be by her/himself. An orange person does not like to hurt anybody and will often leave unnoticed just to avoid confrontation. An orange person feels guilty easily, and a green person knows how to use this. When in balance, they are a very friendly couple. They are both sensitive and like to help people. They are both ruled by their emotions and need to be balanced in order to give each other their best. When in balance, the green person can laugh at the orange person's ideas and stories and even accept the orange person's need to give gifts now and then. In return, the orange person has to understand the green person's crying spells and need for companionship. The orange person must also not run each time something happens that s/he has to take a stand on. The green person needs to feel loved for what s/he is. The green person must get better at helping the orange person gain self-confidence and independence. The green person is on earth to give love and the orange person to give happiness and to heal. Together they can be a wonderful couple, especially if they can work well together.

RELATIONSHIPS GREEN/YELLOW

A yellow person will get along easily with a green person. They will grow in all ways together. The green person's loving and sacrificing ways will be a good support to the impractical and philosophical yellow person. The green person will admire his/her partner's intelligence, good sense of humor, and optimistic view of life. The yellow person will feel comfortable surrounded by the green person's care. Both will be happy with life as it is. When unbalanced, the yellow person becomes selfish and pessimistic. S/he will blame the green person for not being intellectual enough. The green person will seem too simple-minded and kind for the shrewd and skeptical yellow person. The green person will feel emotionally neglected and will complain about not being understood or valued enough.

Green Energy And Why You Are A Green Person

RELATIONSHIPS GREEN/BLUE

This couple has to use all the goodwill and love they have to make their relationship work. The blue person, driven by willpower, is ambitious and goal oriented. The emotion-dominated green person always has his/her partner as a top priority. The green person feels that s/he is

always a lower priority to the blue person. Their philosophies towards life are very different, so even when balanced they have to work hard at making the relationship a success. When unbalanced, the blue person becomes cool and talks sharply to hurt the green person. The green person complains about how little s/he is understood and appreciated.

RELATIONSHIPS GREEN/INDIGO

This is a very emotionally based but strong relationship. These two energies in relationships are warm, loving, and self-sacrificing. It is natural for the green person to support the people s/he loves. And the indigo person needs

the strength from this pure and unselfish love. The green person understands, deep down, the strong spiritual connection the indigo person has to the universe. And the green person wishes for peace and love on earth just as much as the indigo person does. The indigo person needs someone to understand what s/he believes in, without asking for confirmation of facts or details. The green person also understands the depth of love the indigo person seeks–a soul-to-soul connection. When unbalanced and without energy, the indigo person loses a foothold on reality and withdraws into her/himself. If the green person lacks energy, s/he becomes self-pitying and takes on a martyr role. When unbalanced, the green person tries to manipulate through guilt. This is something the indigo person cannot relate to or understand at all. Therefore, it is very important that this combination stays in balance, or the couple will have very little to talk about.

RELATIONSHIPS GREEN/VIOLET

This is a strong couple–the green person with his/her tremendous ability to give unconditional love and the violet person with his/her vision of helping the world. The green person supports and helps the violet person by

trusting in the violet person's dreams and visions. The green person likes and values the unconventional and open violet person. The violet person understands and gives the green person all the deep love s/he need to use all the power s/he has. When unbalanced, the violet person becomes arrogant, self-centred, and self-ish. S/he takes on way too many projects. It easy for the violet person to exploit the green person's helping and caring nature. When unbalanced, the violet person can also readily be unfaithful to his/her partner.

Green Interior Design

Green is a nice balancing colour suitable for waiting rooms and bedrooms. It would also be good in kitchens where there is a lot of daylight, and in workshop areas. Green in all shades is good for hospitals and for rooms where a calming effect is desired. But people who feel they have not been getting anything done during the day or in their lives should not be in green surroundings.

Green Energy Drinks

A glass of green energy drink is beneficial for heart diseases, high or low blood pressure, and headaches.

Green Gemstones

The emerald is the main stone of green people. The green emerald ray will help stabilize disharmonies in the body and mind. Its power is in helping people with their personal development. Everybody who wishes to develop the positive side of the green energy should wear this stone.

Green Food

Green energy is in everything green, such as lettuce, avocados, green beans, broccoli, cucumbers, peas, and zucchinis.

The Green Centre–Organs And Glands

The green chakra is connected to the heart and the nervous system. It influences the thymus gland, which is responsible for the immune system. In stressful situations, it works with the adrenal glands also. The green chakra is connected to the self-preservation instinct and the ability to take care of one's self and one's own health.

Affirmations For Green People

"I need help today from your vast ability to love, your warm caring for others, your helpfulness, and your happy, kind, and generous nature. I need the green energy. I feel green. I am green."

Too Much Green Energy–Overactive

In this situation, the emotions become out of control. One minute the person is sentimental and loving, and the next minute he or she is manipulative and complaining. He or she becomes absorbed with security and with the idea that others should take care of her or him.

Too Little Green Energy–Underactive

The emotions become totally blocked when there is not enough green energy. The heart stops functioning at the emotional level. Greed for material things hinders development of any kind.

Characteristics Of Green People

Positive

Harmonious
Loves children and animals
Loves every living creature
Loves to be loved
Loves to love one person
+ Sensitive
Self-controlled
Adaptable
Sympathetic
Compassionate
Generous
Humble
Happy
Kind
Generous
Likes baking and cooking
Open hearted
Comforting
Neat
Likes to make things
  nice for others
Likes to have company
Likes to have friends
Family orientated
Romantic
Loving

Negative

Lacks judgment
+ Overly materialistic
+ Envious
+ Jealous
Anxious
+ Greedy
Petty
Suspicious
Apathetic
+ Cruel
+ Mean
+ Spiteful
Sloppy
Messy
Gossiper
Talks behind
  people's backs
Creates trouble in
  the family
+ Oversensitive
Cries easily
Pouts easily
Easily despondent
Clingy
Constant complainer
No faith in life
Self-centred
Lacks energy

Blue people ~
Blue sex ~ Blue health ~ Money
and success for blue people ~ Occupations
for blue people ~ Blue children ~ Blue
parents ~ Blue relationships ~ Blue interior
design ~ Blue energy drinks ~ Blue gemstones
~ Blue food ~ The blue centre, organs and
glands ~ Affirmations for blue people ~ Blue
energy, overactive and underactive
~ Blue positive and
negative

BLUE ENERGY AND
WHY YOU ARE A BLUE PERSON

Blue People

Blue people are people of will. A blue person has a great urge to succeed. Blue people exude a sense of security and trust. Moreover, blue people trust their own energy. Blue people have the ability to plan and think strategically. They see cohesion and totality in every project. They also have the ability to identify with the company or organization they work for. Blue people are born leaders and politicians. They gather their life energy by completing their goals. They are career and status people. They are good in situations where self-control is needed. They can be like chameleons in their own world. They have the ability to know exactly how to act around certain people. They are often well-dressed and stylish. They exude peace and order as well as self-control. They make everything seem simple and great. They are natural organizers and rational thinkers. They see things clearly and precisely and know how to realize ideas. The blue person's overall favorite activity is creative problem solving. Blue people are more interested in ideas and projects than people, but when they feel that they are accepted for other things besides their logical thinking, they will open up and become warm and extremely nice to be with. Blue people are in control of their feelings all the time. Marriage is often a calculated action on their part. They try to find a socially presentable partner who will take care of the home and family for them or they try to find someone who is as intelligent as they are. When unbalanced, blue people become sarcastic and think that everybody else is stupid. This feeling of superiority can easily lead to a misuse of power. Unbalanced blue people also plan their lives according to their image of how successful people should live. They hide their emotions and become controlling. They think that to fail and to experience downfalls is unacceptable. When unbalanced, they overestimate themselves and think that everything they do is right. Furthermore, they blame others and jump ship only to throw themselves into another project.

Blue Sex

Blue people enjoy sex as long as it is not too passionate. When a blue person lacks energy or if something is wrong in the relationship, s/he uses sex as a means of manipulating his/her partner and getting what s/he wants. A blue person can refuse their partner sex until s/he gets what s/he wants. The blue person frequently lets business or other important things come before sex. It is never easy for a partner to be second in line. Sex is meant to join people together, not to divide them.

Blue Health

When blue people are in balance, they are powerful and healthy. They do not use their physical bodies much and therefore often have cold hands and feet. Their biggest weakness is in the throat area, because they suppress their feelings. If you swallow hurt feelings and tears too often, the body will react at some point. Their biggest problem is learning to relax. The only time blue people truly relax is when they are totally in control of their lives. Blue people can help themselves by making lists, learning to establish priorities, and not setting too many or too high goals. Blue people feel important when they are very busy, and when they feel that what they are doing really counts. This creates a lot of stress. Blue people have to learn that they do not have to control everything in life. They have to learn to breathe deeply. Then they will think more rationally and clearly.

Stiff shoulders and neck indicate, typically, that the blue person has to relax. When the blue person's throat becomes hoarse, thick, and irritable it indicates that s/he cannot express what s/he wants to express. Learning to relax is one of the best ways of staying healthy. People are so busy with work, social engagements, and activities that their days are very hectic. If activities occupy more than twelve hours of the day, the body and soul do not have time enough to get to know each other. People need to sit down and listen to their bodies and the signals they send. When people do not listen to their bodies, physical illnesses can occur to indicate that something is wrong. Usually there is a psychological reason behind a symptom that becomes an illness.

Money And Success For Blue People

Blue people easily acquire money, but they work hard for the money too. Money means status, power, and security. They have an inner power, that helps them to acquire nice things and money easily. Blue people judge their success by what they have obtained in life, by how much people respect them, or by how much money they have.

Occupations For Blue People

Blue people are good business people, teachers, historians, missionaries, art collectors, politicians, preachers, ministers, religious leaders, singers, archaeologists, church assistants, entrepreneurs, bankers, corporate heads, real estate agents, and stock brokers. They make good nurses and landlords too. Blue people are generally good in any profession that requires organization, order, and control.

Blue Children

Blue children are very intelligent. They learn fast and ask a lot of questions. They have strong willpower. It is not long before they start to challenge and order around their parents. Blue children come across as being very mature, because they master language at an early age. Blue children like it if you listen to what they are saying and if you respect them for their opinions. They easily become frustrated. They scream and disrupt conversations just to get attention. This can be very difficult for parents if they do not understand their children and the needs they have. Blue children learn best if goals are challenging and if they can use logic to solve problems. Parents should teach blue children not to be afraid of making mistakes. Blue children are good in school and always complete their education.

Blue Parents

Blue people organize their parental responsibilities. They wish the best for their children—a good education and the best after-school activities. Blue people often wait to have children until they have a stable home and are financially secure. When the child is an infant, they prefer to have help with childcare. They organize their lives around their children and support them financially. They often forget that they are dealing with children, not small adults. When blue parents are well balanced they teach by example, but if blue parents lack energy, they have difficulty giving anything positive to their children. They oppress their children by being arrogant and overly critical.

Blue Relationships

A blue person needs a good relationship, but only if it is of a certain standard. The blue person needs somebody s/he can respect and who will work towards the same goals the blue person has set for her/himself. Blue people often choose their friends carefully because of their workaholic tendencies and goal orientation. Blue people need strong and independent partners to support them as they have all their willpower focused on goals. When blue people lack energy, they often become the victim of their own perfectionism. Blue people then become easily frustrated and blame other people or their environment for the circumstances they are in. Blue people are very vocal when frustrated and can seem arrogant, offensive, and belligerent. It is very difficult to satisfy blue people when they are unbalanced. Fortunately blue people are very strong-willed and intelligent, so they can easily reestablish balance if they really want to.

RELATIONSHIPS BLUE/BLUE

This is a strongly success-oriented and ambitious couple. The couple is very stable financially. Both people strive for power and status. Two blue people have to respect each other and should not challenge each other. They both like to be right and do not easily accept losing an argument. If they have their own businesses or if they are both specialists in their own fields, the relationship will do fine, as long as they admire each other and respect each other's work. Problems arise if one person wants to dominate the other. Blue people cannot stand being controlled. If they want the relationship to last, they will have to make compromises and make an effort to respect each other. Blue people need to respect and admire their partners. Money, high status positions, and beautiful homes often characterize these relationships. When in balance, the two people give each other courage and stimulate each other to learn and develop more. If they are unbalanced or if they have not developed respect for each other, they can become incredibly mean to each other. Since they are very intelligent and verbally skillful, their arguments often will be exciting and stimulating.

RELATIONSHIPS BLUE/RED

This can be a very dynamic couple. The blue person's ability to plan and organize combined with the red person's ability to realize plans is an outstanding combination. A red person sees the opportunity to realize plans as a wonderful challenge. The strong power that drives a red person fascinates a blue person. The blue person admires and values the red person's perseverance and will to go through with the hard challenges s/he takes on, while the red person admires the blue person's intelligence, mental strength, and ability to express her/himself. When balanced, they are each other's best support. The blue person needs the red person's fire and drive, and the red person needs the blue person's mental calmness. They are a very lively and outgoing couple with much respect for each other. But if they are unbalanced, they both have problems controlling their tempers. A red person can have a furious, uncontrollable temper. The blue person uses his/her sharp tongue to provoke the red person who will then quickly lose control over her/himself. The blue person does not hesitate to lay blame on the red person. Both people are strong willed and will want the last word in a fight.

RELATIONSHIPS BLUE/ORANGE

This can be a challenging relationship. They will learn a tremendous amount from each other, because they do not share the same standards or goals. The blue person is good at realizing ideas and plans and will be inspired by the vital and creative orange person. The blue person is a great manager while the orange person is an artist. As long as this couple is in balance, they complement each other's talents. The couple then has the potential of going far in life together. The blue person needs admiration and respect from other people. And this is the best thing the orange person can give his/her partner. Since a blue person teaches by example, an orange person learns easily from her or him. The orange person hates to be told what to do.

If unbalanced, the orange person will feel oppressed by a blue partner. The orange person then works her/himself up and provokes the blue partner. In response, an unbalanced blue person will verbally abuse the orange person back. Verbal abuse is something an orange person cannot defend her/himself against. The orange person has to understand that a blue person lives life differently. Blue people often feel frustrated and irritated by their own behavior. They are perfectionists and have a hard time living up to their own standards. The orange person can help the blue person to take life a little less seriously and teach the blue person to laugh at herself or himself. Admiration and respect is the best gift a blue person can receive from an orange person.

RELATIONSHIPS BLUE/YELLOW

Again this is a good relationship, especially at the intellectual level. The yellow person with his/her knowledge, intellectual pursuits, sense of humor, and kindness stimulates and interests the blue person. The blue person will inspire the yellow person with his/her wisdom and ability to reach goals. This relationship enables both partners to grow and to develop new ideas in areas such as research, teaching methods, politics, and inventions. Anything will be possible in this relationship. When unbalanced, they lose faith in each other and become pessimistic and negative. The blue person becomes sarcastic and says hurtful things. The yellow person acts in cowardly way, avoiding any confrontation.

RELATIONSHIPS BLUE/GREEN

This couple has to use all the goodwill and love they have to make their relationship work. The blue person, driven by willpower, is ambitious and goal oriented. The emotion-dominated green person always has his/her partner as a top priority. The green person feels that s/he is always a lower priority to the blue person. Their philosophies towards life are very different, so even when balanced they have to work hard at making the relationship a success. When unbalanced, the blue person becomes cool and talks sharply to hurt the green person. The green person complains about how little s/he is understood and appreciated.

RELATIONSHIPS BLUE/INDIGO

These two people are fascinated with each other at a very special level. The blue person finds the indigo's thoughts and ideas really interesting. The indigo person is very curious about the intelligent and well-informed blue person. The blue person is the dominant one in the relationship basically because the blue person is more strong-willed and has a flair for money and success. The indigo emotion-dominated person has no knack for finances. But the indigo person becomes defiant if an unbalanced blue person is irresponsible or fraudulent with money. This is against the indigo person's principles, and s/he will resist the blue person's attempt to gain control. When well balanced, they are an extremely effective couple. They help each other to grow and to gain knowledge.

RELATIONSHIPS BLUE/VIOLET

If balanced, this couple can be dynamic, productive, and harmonious. This relationship can be the most financially prosperous and successful of all the colour energy combinations. They both have a flair for money. The blue person likes to make money with the violet person, because the violet person has so many good ideas. The blue person uses his/her organizational skills to realize the violet person's ideas. The violet person does not have any problem with letting the blue person be powerful and domineering. S/he will go his/her own way regardless of what the blue person says or does. The violet person has goals with a higher meaning at work. The violet person likes money because of the freedom it gives her/him to travel and be philanthropic. When balanced, ideally the blue person supports and organizes the violet person's ideas. When unbalanced, the blue person does not have confidence in the violet person's ideas. The blue person wants proof, facts, and numbers, and criticizes the violet person for being an unrealistic dreamer. If unbalanced, the violet person leads a disorganized life and engages in many frivolous private and business relationships. This behavior will irritate the organized blue partner.

Blue Interior Design

This is a peaceful and calming colour. It is good for bedrooms, waiting rooms, and offices. It would be a bit too cold for dining rooms, but in kitchens it can be a good balance to the warm activity of cooking. Blue is a very relaxing colour, and too much of it can lead to melancholy and laziness.

Blue Energy Drinks

Blue energy drinks can help sore throats, hoarseness, fever, jaundice, abrasions, burns, and rheumatism.

Blue Gemstones

The main gemstone of blue people is the sapphire. People who work in an intellectually stimulating environment can draw on this stone for strength. Ideas are created constantly. A minute hardly passes by without new ideas popping up. The sapphire helps keep thoughts organized and helps sort out unnecessary thoughts so you can concentrate on what is important. The sapphire can help you to increase your self-control of body, mind, and soul.

Blue Food

There is beneficial blue energy in blueberries, dewberries, plums, rosehips, pears, celery, asparagus, and potatoes. Chicken, veal, and fish are blue foods as well.

The Blue Centre–Organs And Glands

The blue chakra is connected to the throat and the pharynx centre. The pharynx centre regulates the thyroid and the parathyroid glands. The main hormone produced by these glands is tyrosine. Tyrosine regulates the homeostasis of the whole body. It also regulates the metabolic processes. Furthermore, it regulates the intake of energy through the food we eat and the air we breathe. The blue centre affects our ability to communicate and the development of our vocal chords. The sound of our voice reveals how developed our throat chakra is. The blue centre also helps to develop leadership abilities.

Affirmations For Blue People
"Today I need help from your clear, broad-minded, and mentally creative energy. I need calmness in my thoughts to organize and plan my activities. I need your power so that my communication is clear and my thoughts pure. I need blue energy. I feel blue. I am blue."

Too Much Blue Energy–Overactive
If blue energy is overactive in a person, he or she talks nervously and uncontrollably all the time and tries to manipulate people. Desire for power and fame can run out of control too.

Too Little Blue Energy–Underactive
If a person has underactive blue energy, he or she talks too little and too softly. Such people are afraid of expressing themselves, both verbally and emotionally, and tend to blush and cough to hide their feelings. A poor self-image is connected to an underactive throat chakra.

Characteristic Of Blue People

Positive

Broad-minded
Clear-sighted
Faithful
Loyal
Tactful
Affectionate
Inspirational
Innovative
Mentally imaginative
Mentally creative
Ability to organize
Ability to plan
Ability to be
 a natural leader
Ability to be
verbally skillful
Ability to organize
 time well
Ability to organize
 your own power
Ability to be
 financially responsible
Ability to be diplomatic
Art and beauty lover
Art collector
+ Self-controlled
Calm
Mentally persevering
Stable
Nostalgic
Patient
Content
Idealistic
Authoritative

Negative

Over ambitious
Distrusting
Lacking in
 confidence
Suspicious
+ Critical
Apathetic
+ Snobbish
Unorganized
+ Scheming
+ Calculating
+ Cold
Pedantic
Lacking in control
Intellectually
 scattered
Talkative
Repetitive
+ Sarcastic
+ Domineering
+ Feels superior
+ Power seeking
+ Mentally cruel
+ Insensitive
+ Patronizing
+ Self-satisfied
+ Authoritarian
Dogmatic
Stubborn
Ultra-conservative
Reacts slowly
+ Fanatical
Skeptical of change
+ Arrogant
Hung-up on details

Indigo people ~
Indigo sex ~Indigo health ~
Money and success for indigo people ~
Occupations for indigo people ~Indigo
children~Indigo parents~Indigo relationships
~Indigo interior design ~Indigo energy drinks
~ Indigo gemstones ~ Indigo food ~The indigo
centre, organs and glands ~Affirmations for
indigo people ~Indigo energy, overactive
and underactive ~Indigo positive
and negative

INDIGO ENERGY AND WHY YOU ARE AN INDIGO PERSON

Indigo People

Nowadays more indigo people are being born than ever before, as the time is right for this energy. People want to explore their spiritual dimension. Indigo people are the leaders and the guides in this area, because they understand humankind's place in the world. They know that everyone is a part of the whole universe. Indigo people are passionate in their own way. They work towards a higher goal. They want to teach people how to reach their own inner universe, their souls. We are intuitive because our bodies are a biochemical system that feels and understands waves and vibrations, almost like a technical instrument. Indigo people are intuitive, and they absorb so much information all the time that they get tired quickly. Their tiredness is often mistaken for inattention or laziness. Indigo people are bright and inquisitive. They have an intelligence that cannot be tested the usual way. They basically know everything intuitively, and only seek to confirm this knowledge or feeling.

Indigo people are naturally concerned with the environment. They easily think in ecological terms. Their world is the unknown–the world of dreams and symbols. They are often recognized by what they are wearing. Like violet people, indigo people use clothes to emphasize their independence. Black, indigo, and purple colours–often in strange variations–are used to express the melancholic and frequently depressed nature of indigo people. This way of dressing is more typical when indigo people are unbalanced. On the other hand, if indigo people have too much indigo energy, they wear colourful and totally outlandish outfits. When balanced, indigo people have little interest in their body and clothes. Indigo energy is a difficult energy to balance, because we have so little knowledge and understanding about the world of thought it represents. There are psychologists and psychiatrists who deal with people who have lost touch with reality, and for those the psychologists cannot help, there are mental institutions. But the best course of action would be to intervene before people end up as patients.

Clairvoyants have shown that many unknown energies exist that we can use. And nowadays the indigo energy is being researched at the same level as other energies. We are headed for an indigo age. But it probably will not help indigo people in the near future. Indigo people must try to stay balanced and complete what they have to do on earth. They have to trust themselves to stay balanced. They should place their feet solidly on the ground and stick to down-to-earth things.

Indigo people always tell the truth no matter how cruel and brutal it may be. They are not ruled by the usual standards of good manners. They look at the negative and positive sides as a whole, and therefore they do not feel blame or shame. Most people on the other hand were raised to hide the truth. When indigo people say no, they mean no. They often have difficulty in relationships, as they have to be liked and loved for what they are. When indigo people are balanced they cannot change, even though other people try to change them. When balanced, indigo people are true to themselves. It is by being true to themselves that they teach others to be true to their inner selves as well. This is the goal of the indigo energy.

Indigo Sex
For indigo people, sex is a deep spiritual event between two people. The indigo person cannot have sex without feeling deep love. Indigo people usually have integrated the female and male sides of themselves. Therefore, they do not need sex to feel whole or to feel the togetherness of a sexual relationship. To the indigo person, sex is a cosmic union. If the indigo person is unbalanced, sex is something he or she uses as an escape.

Indigo Health
When in balance, indigo people intuitively understand that the physical body is more than a biochemical machine. It is alive with energy. Consequently, they know how to cure their own illnesses by adjusting their thought patterns. When unbalanced, indigo people forget these principles and become ill. The indigo person will feel divided between his/her own physical body and his/her own inner eye or universal body.

The biggest health concern for indigo people is mental illness. They have very few people with whom they can communicate. If in a negative state of mind, they are very susceptible to viruses and depression. The best way indigo people can help themselves is by following their true nature and by regaining their balance. Prayers and meditation help them do this. Indigo people fall through the cracks of the system, and become burdens to society if they do not find a constructive meaning to life and a connection to the source of life.

The indigo energy, more than any other energy, is the energy of our time. Many children are being born with indigo energy nowadays. Indigo people are here on earth to teach us that we are responsible for our own health. Illnesses of the physical body reflect what little control we have over ourselves. We create our own illnesses from what we think, do, eat, and live. Our illnesses are the result of how we live and how we confront our lives. We show who we are through our illnesses.

Health Tips For Indigo People
Indigo people can develop serious health problems, if the people they love and trust betray and lie to them. This is especially true if the indigo person first finds out about the deception through their intuition.

Money And Success For Indigo People
Indigo people understand that money is energy and that you need money in this world to survive. Indigo people, like green and violet people, cannot work for financial gain only. They would never do anything that would harm people, plants, or the environment for financial gain. As idealists, they would rather die. They feel successful and happy when they can do what they want to do and believe in what they will. They feel that they have succeeded when they can help other souls and when humanity seems to be on the right track. Indigo people's goal is the sense of universal connection and community.

Occupations For Indigo People
Indigo people choose employment in which they can influence other people with their faith. This includes child-related jobs, social work, and all animal-related work. Indigo people make good artists, designers, writers, composers, musicians, counselors, parapsychologists, and clairvoyants.

Indigo Children
Indigo children seek the truth in everything. It is difficult for parents when their children have their own standards and laws for what is right and wrong, especially when the children refuse to be disciplined. Indigo children must have peace to

develop according to their own rhythm. They are very inquisitive and do not accept answers such as "that is just the way it is." These children can easily be misunderstood. They are not being difficult or stubborn. They are just so eager to know what is behind everything or what is the truth. Indigo children do not need much sleep. They are often alone, because many people find it hard to understand these extremely sensitive children.

Indigo Parents

Sensitive indigo parents feel that they do not own their children and that they are here to help the children understand who they are. They feel that they have a responsibility to teach their children all they can. It can be very difficult for indigo parents, who have an inner security and belief to hold on to, when their children will not learn what they feel is right. Indigo parents do not believe in discipline and physical punishment. They believe in love and mutual respect.

Indigo Relationships

Indigo people need partners who will support them and give them security in their faith. They have a special belief system that cannot be explained or supported by logic or facts. Their partners are their best friends first of all and only secondarily their lovers. They are loyal and monogamous partners. They need security and trust from their partners, so they can rely on their special belief-system and thought-system for the future. They have a very hard time emotionally, if they believe that their partners have lost faith in them. Without enough energy, indigo people can become lost. They need a fixed point or goal in life. Without this it can be very difficult for them to relate to life on earth. They will often withdraw into their own world. At least there they are safe.

RELATIONSHIPS INDIGO/INDIGO

This couple should be just friends rather than lovers. They are both dominated by their emotions. Because of this, they understand each other fully. Moreover, since neither of them is strong-willed, they do not try to control each other. They are not a grounded couple, as it is hard  for them to relate to the practical and physical world. Indigo people really need someone to take charge and look after them. It is better if indigo people find other partners.

Indigo Energy And Why You Are An Indigo Person

RELATIONSHIPS INDIGO/RED

These are two extremely different personalities—the physical and grounded red person and the ethereal or esoteric indigo person with little or no relationship to his/her physical body. The indigo person is so introverted and sensitive that s/he has difficulty relating to the red person's extroverted and explosive energy. They are only alike when it comes to their natural relationship to solitude and to working alone. They will constantly misunderstand each other in discussions or conversations. They are miles apart when it comes to understanding problems or situations.

RELATIONSHIPS INDIGO/ORANGE

Orange and indigo people make good friends. The orange person's attitude towards play and happiness fascinates the indigo person, just as the indigo person's attitude to the other world attracts the orange person. They both are dominated by emotional energies and are fascinated by people and human relations. They both wish to be liked by other people. They are both stubborn and like to do their own thing. While the indigo person strives for a soul-to-soul relationship, the orange person seeks a carefree, no-obligation relationship. The orange person lives in the here-and-now and is not looking for a soul mate. If balanced, they will gain a lot from each other. They can teach each other about life as seen from two different perspectives—the indigo person with his/her spiritual focus and the orange person's focus on earthly pleasures. If unbalanced, it is likely that they will not be able to help each other much. The indigo person will lose confidence in the irresponsible orange person, and the orange person will accuse the indigo person of being flaky and living in a dreamland. An unbalanced indigo person will constantly have identity crises. Indigo people lose their balance quickly. An unbalanced orange person will not be able to provide the support the indigo person needs. The orange person will have no self-confidence and will be full of fear. The indigo person and orange person are then a couple in which the blind try to lead the blind.

RELATIONSHIPS INDIGO/ YELLOW

This couple can do well together if they are both balanced. They are both naturally helpful. They both seek the truth—the yellow person through philosophy and theories, and the indigo person through an inner belief system—yet, each respects the other's differences. Financially they are comfortable, but their cheque books never balance. An indigo person feels happy with a positive yellow person, mostly because the yellow person is intelligent and well informed about things. The yellow person also tolerates people and is not judgmental. When unbalanced, they both withdraw into themselves. The indigo person lives in his/her inner world. The yellow person turns his/her skepticism and pessimism against the world and retreats.

RELATIONSHIPS INDIGO/GREEN

This is a very emotionally based but strong relationship. These two energies in relationships are warm, loving, and self-sacrificing. It is natural for the green person to support the people s/he loves. And the indigo person needs the strength from this pure and unselfish love. The green person understands, deep down, the strong spiritual connection the indigo person has to the universe. And the green person wishes peace and love on earth just as much as the indigo person does. The indigo person needs someone to understand what s/he believes in, without asking for confirmation of facts or details. The green person also understands the depth of love the indigo person seeks–a soul-to-soul connection. When unbalanced and without energy, the indigo person loses a foothold on reality and withdraws into her/himself. If the green person lacks energy, s/he becomes self-pitying and takes on a martyr role. When unbalanced, the green person tries to manipulate through guilt. This is something the indigo person cannot relate to or understand at all. Therefore, it is very important that this combination stays in balance, or the couple will have very little to talk about.

RELATIONSHIPS INDIGO/BLUE

These two people are fascinated with each other at a very special level. The blue person finds the indigo's thoughts and ideas really fascinating. The indigo person is very curious about the intelligent and well-informed blue person. The blue person is the dominant one in the relationship basically because the blue person is more strong-willed and has a flair for money and success. The indigo emotion-dominated person has no knack for finances. But the indigo person becomes defiant if an unbalanced blue person is irresponsible or fraudulent with money. This is against the indigo person's principles, and s/he will resist the blue person's attempt to gain control. When well balanced, they are an extremely effective couple. They help each other to grow and to gain knowledge.

RELATIONSHIPS INDIGO/VIOLET

This is an exciting and highly developed couple. They can be pure visionaries and pioneers. They both are interested in people and cultures and love to travel. They seek truth and a higher connection to the universe. They work for peace and the spiritual development of this planet. The violet person's strong leadership qualities and the indigo person's highly intuitive mind and belief-system have the potential of uniting in art and other forms of expression. The violet person's need to be the centre of attention does not have to compete with the subdued indigo personality. An unbalanced violet person tries to dominate an indigo partner. The indigo person does not understand this. If the situation becomes too annoying, the indigo person will leave the relationship. When balanced, each person gathers strength from the other. The indigo person gets all his/her questions answered. The violet person receives inspiration to do the things s/he needs to do.

Indigo Interior Design

A pastel indigo is perfect for bedrooms and treatment rooms. However, the colour is not suitable for rooms where people with psychiatric problems are being cared for. Alcoholics and drug addicts should avoid this colour. This colour contains many negative aspects. Delirium and compulsive ideas are closely connected to indigo.

Indigo Energy Drinks

An indigo drink will help with sleeping problems, hearing problems, eye cataracts, eye and ear infections, and mental illnesses. A glass every day will help the body's system in a general way.

Indigo Gemstones

Quartz crystals are the main stone for indigo people. Quartz crystals are alive and therefore very powerful. They have concentrated energy stored in layers. This energy connection with the universe and the earth is very helpful for indigo people. Quartz crystals are a very effective therapeutic tool. They can be placed along the spine to increase the energy of life. Broken or sprained leg muscles will greatly benefit from quartz crystals.

Indigo Food
There is indigo colour energy in eggplants, broccoli, blue grapes, and all indigo coloured food.

The Indigo Centre–Organs And Glands
We often call the indigo chakra the third eye. It is the organ for inner sight. This centre is connected to the bone marrow and the nervous system. It influences the pineal gland, which is the master conductor. This centre also incarnates super sensitivity and the ability to reach universal consciousness.

Affirmations For Indigo People
"Today I need help from your intuitive, truth seeking power and your fearless, honest attitude towards life and death. I need to feel and know that I am part of a greater whole and that I am not alone. I need the indigo energy. I feel indigo. I am indigo."

Too Much Indigo–Overactive
When someone wishes to increase his or her consciousness beyond their current threshold, it can lead to an opening in the brow chakra that is too big. Many people who have an overactive brow chakra are admitted to psychiatric institutions with anxiety attacks, hallucinations, delusions, and psychosis. They have lost contact with their physical bodies and live in another reality.

Too Little Indigo–Underactive
In this situation people have little contact with their intuition and with the other six energies. They float around without anything to hold on to. They are afraid of using their intuition and of losing the last grip that holds them to the earth.

Characteristics Of Indigo People

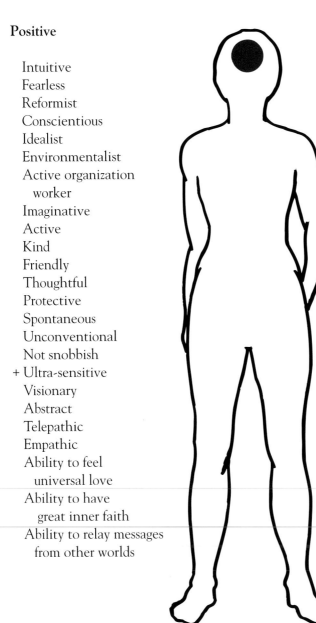

Positive

Intuitive
Fearless
Reformist
Conscientious
Idealist
Environmentalist
Active organization
  worker
Imaginative
Active
Kind
Friendly
Thoughtful
Protective
Spontaneous
Unconventional
Not snobbish
+ Ultra-sensitive
Visionary
Abstract
Telepathic
Empathic
Ability to feel
  universal love
Ability to have
  great inner faith
Ability to relay messages
  from other worlds

Negative

Timid
+ Intolerant
Impractical
+ Judgmental
Sad
Depressed
Suicidal
Passive
Compulsion to
  avoid things
Not practical
Drug addict
Alcoholic
Self-centred
Absent-minded
Afraid
Lacking in faith
Lacking in trust
Alienated
Inefficient
Forgetful
Undisciplined
Introverted
Imprecise
Unsuccessful
Fears the future
Unable to live in
  the present
Remote
Not in touch with
  reality

Violet people ~
Violet sex ~ Violet health ~
Money and success for violet people ~
Occupations for violet people ~ Violet
children ~ Violet parents ~ Violet relationships
~ Violet interior design ~ Violet energy drinks ~
Violet gemstones ~ Violet food ~ The violet centre,
organs and glands ~ Affirmations for violet
people ~ Violet energy, overactive and
underactive ~ Violet positive
and negative

VIOLET ENERGY AND WHY YOU ARE A VIOLET PERSON

Violet People

Violet people are linked to the emotional and spiritual balance of the world. They have energy resources that they can use collectively to influence humankind. The violet energy creates saints, global leaders, great artists, and heralds for a new world. Violet people are visionaries. They foresee the future, because they understand and are able to see the fruits of what others have planted. Violet people are exceptionally intelligent. They are critical thinkers as well as creative idea makers. They are often seen as too critical because they use a complex system to judge and evaluate situations in their own and other people's lives and point out all the mistakes. They often feel frustrated over the fact that others cannot see or imagine all sides of a case as clearly as they can. Therefore, research type work is ideal for them. They are theorists, interested in creating hypotheses and models for ideas, but not very interested in realizing their theories. It is the idea that counts. They often come across as cool, arrogant, secure, and strong. They give the impression that they like themselves very much, but it is not always so. They often doubt themselves, mostly because they are always one step ahead of others. Being future oriented and ahead of their time causes them to feel lonely, thus they often build walls around themselves as protection.

Violet people are very sensitive and intuitive. They seem to have an understanding of all old teachings and gather strength and ideas from these sources. They are idealists and lovers of beauty, and they like to surround themselves with beautiful things that have harmony and balance. Violet people are attracted to all beautiful things that have life-energy. Violet people often feel an urge, almost a calling, to be missionaries of some kind, but they often feel that they neither have the knowledge nor the experience to complete what they are going to do. They feel that they do not have a choice, that the goal they are aiming for has nothing to do with their own need for attention but is something they have to do. They are good leaders because they have so much power, but their leadership seems at times almost dictatorial. They tell people what to do. When a violet person works with inspiration and vision, there are few people who do not submit to their dictatorial style. When unbalanced, their leadership qualities become domineering, and in the end they lose control.

When in a negative state, violet people become self-centred and selfish. It is the positive violet energy that makes things happen. Others may think that violet people are very concerned with money. It can seem that way, but violet people think of money and success as power, and they need the power money represents to realize their ideas and to motivate and inspire others.

When unbalanced, violet people try to arrange their lives in a certain direction or life-style. For example, they will have Bohemian furnishings, clothes, and friends. Melancholic music and conversations about life and death until the early hours of the morning, accompanied by a glass of red wine, complete the pattern. Violet people are charismatic. They are here on earth to raise people's spiritual awareness. They want people to know that where there is spiritual consciousness, everyday and ordinary events and things can be lifted to a higher sphere. Everything, from exercise and art to speeches and actions, has the potential to be transformed by this spiritual consciousness. If violet energy is not used in a positive way, it will demand some sort of an outlet. At this point, it is easy for the violet energy to use sex to blow off steam.

Violet Sex

Violet people are charismatic. They have sex appeal and a strong sexual appetite. Unless they are busy with things that interest them more, they are easily led into sexual liaisons. This can be unfortunate if the violet person is in a monogamous relationship, because infidelity is a sad way to end a relationship. Violet people need sex. If they do not get their needs met, they become frustrated. It is in this situation that infidelity occurs. Violet people are passionate in their sex lives and sexually proficient. It is important that violet people understand that when they are frustrated and sex is used to compensate, it is because they are not continuing their own development. Violet people have to continue their development, and not rely on sex as their only fulfillment. Many homosexual violet people have totally lost contact with what life is about and with what life demands of each and every person. Instead they have based their world on sexual fulfillment. This is a waste of valuable energy, which should be used for a totally different purpose than personal satisfaction.

Violet Health

Violet people have either fully charged energy levels or very low energy levels. Their life energy can be easily frittered away. They have to learn how to concentrate their energy on one or two projects. They usually have too many projects going on at one time. Meditation and Tai-Chi can help them find their balance. Illnesses always affect them when they are low in energy. Violet people should focus on specific tasks and keep their energy under control.

Money And Success For Violet People

The wealthiest people on the planet are blue and violet. The difference between the two is that blue people can work for money only, while violet people must believe in what they work for. They must enjoy their work and be certain that there is a higher purpose behind their success. To know success, violet people must feel that they have touched the world with their message. They must feel that they have done their share in making this world a better place to live. Violet people contribute much to society, whether they are great artists or great leaders. You seldom have any doubts when you run into a violet person. They are very charismatic.

Occupations For Violet People

Violet people are happiest when they are self- employed. They find it difficult to work for others. Media technology plays an important part in violet people's lives; they can reach a larger audience through television, film, or theatre. Violet people often work as writers, teachers, politicians, astronauts, psychologists, architects, or designers. Artists, leaders, and messengers of the world benefit from the violet energy's inspiring power.

Violet Children

Violet children are born leaders and other children feel drawn to them. They are full of energy. When in balance, they will care for their friends. They are very sexually oriented from childhood and experiment sexually with themselves. It is natural for violet children to do this. Parents must not condemn this or discipline their children for this behavior, or the children will grow up thinking that it is wrong to express themselves sexually. Violet children can see auras, angels, spirits, and other dimensions. Parents should let them talk about what they see and not dismiss it as the result of an overactive imagination. They should teach the children to have faith in what they see. It is very important that parents teach these active children to concentrate and limit their activities without dampening their interests. Some children show leadership qualities and idealism at an early age. They often will become scoutmasters or take on other leadership roles in idealistic organizations.

Violet Parents

Violet parents do not become emotionally involved with their children. They believe that children develop best without interference. Their children have to find their own way. Usually violet parents are so busy with their own lives that they do not have much time left over for their children. They have so much to do. Remember, they have to help save the world. When unbalanced, violet parents become dictatorial and do not accept any kind of opposition. They can become so absorbed in their own activities that they prefer to leave the upbringing and responsibility of their children to other family members or to send their children to boarding schools.

Violet Relationships

Violet people like to be in a relationship but it is not always easy, as everything must be done their way. Violet people want their partners to share their vision and their path. Their partners must be good travel companions and share their enthusiasm. Violet people are sensitive and accept, more than any other type of person, the different ways people express themselves. But the partner still has to submit to the violet person's goals in life. Violet people have an inspirational relationship to the universe; therefore, they have an easygoing view of earthly life. In other words, they belong to the universe and not the Earth. When lacking energy, violet people can lose their way. They throw themselves into too many projects. They see too many possibilities and will not let go of any. It is important for violet people to be balanced. Their energy is very strong-willed.

RELATIONSHIPS VIOLET/VIOLET

This is an extremely powerful couple. They are both charismatic and dynamic. They like music, sex, traveling, and humanitarian work. They have common interests but seldom have the time to be together. In their falling-in-love period they are drawn to each other like magnets. Their love is passionate and all-important. They both have many projects and ideas, but they have difficulty helping each other realize them. Violet people love to be the centre of attention. Therefore, this couple are frequently to be found in the entertainment business.

RELATIONSHIPS VIOLET/RED

This is an interesting combination. The violet person has strong leadership qualities and has a great ability to see into the future. The red person is inspired by this and can help to realize the violet person's ideas. They are both independent and strong-willed. The violet person's head and mind are always in the clouds, while the red person has both feet on the ground. The violet person has deep feelings and is able to express them. Red people also have deep feelings, but they cannot express themselves except in emotional outbursts. When they are both in balance, they are able to work well together as a team. The violet person is able to see all the good qualities of the red person. When unbalanced, the violet person orders the red person around. The red person does not like this at all. In the same way, the red person thinks that the violet person's ideas and thoughts are unrealistic, and thus s/he does not respect the violet person. Because the red person has a realistic attitude, it can be very difficult for the red person to relate to the violet person's way of foreseeing the future. The red person will often be skeptical about what the violet person "sees."

RELATIONSHIPS VIOLET/ORANGE

Orange and violet people can have a lot of fun together. They are both creative and inspire each other. The violet person understands and respects the orange person's need for happiness, play, and freedom. They are both happy when they socialize. They both like unconventional and improvised forms of parties. They both have enormous energy resources and enjoy sex. Usually, the violet person is the leader in the relationship as s/he has drive and an intuitive understanding of the purpose and meaning of life. When in balance, these two have a lot of common interests—music, entertainment, sex, travel, physical exercise, and people. They experience life together and complement each other fully. To others, they seem like a very harmonious and dynamic couple. If unbalanced, the orange person seems lazy, preoccupied, and irresponsible. The violet person will become frustrated and disappointed with an orange partner who is unfaithful, irresponsible with money, and comforts her/himself through substance abuse. The violet person, on the other hand, can become so arrogant and act so superior that the orange person is intimidated and loses his/her self-confidence.

Violet Energy And Why You Are A Violet Person

RELATIONSHIPS VIOLET/YELLOW

This is a good connection. The yellow person is stimulated by the creative and intelligent violet person and
inspired by the violet person's spiritual orientation. The
violet person is inspired by the yellow person's theoretical
and philosophical orientation. The violet person can also be very
artistic. In this case, the yellow person supports the violet partner with optimism
and confidence in the violet person's new ideas and ideals. When unbalanced, the
violet person's spiritual inspiration can easily turn to the occult and black magic.
This is something the yellow person has difficulty understanding. If the yellow person lacks energy, s/he becomes pessimistic and negative and does not make an
effort to solve shared problems.

RELATIONSHIPS VIOLET/GREEN

This is a strong couple—the green person with his/her
tremendous ability to give unconditional love and the
violet person with his/her vision of helping the world.
The green person supports and helps the violet person by
trusting in the violet person's dreams and visions. The green person likes and values the unconventional and open violet person. The violet person understands
and gives the green person all the deep love s/he need to use all the power s/he
has. When unbalanced, the violet person becomes arrogant, self-centred, and selfish. S/he takes on way too many projects. It easy for the violet person to exploit
the green person's helping and caring nature. When unbalanced, the violet person
can also readily be unfaithful to his/her partner.

RELATIONSHIPS VIOLET/BLUE

If balanced, this couple can be dynamic, productive, and
harmonious. This relationship can be the most financial-
ly prosperous and successful of all the colour energy combi-
nations. They both have a flair for money. The blue person
likes to make money with the violet person, because the violet person has so many
good ideas. The blue person uses his/her organizational skills to realize the violet
person's ideas. The violet person does not have any problem with letting the blue
person be powerful and domineering. S/he will go his/her own way regardless of
what the blue person says or does. The violet person has goals with a higher meaning at work. The violet person likes money because of the freedom it gives her/him
to travel and be philanthropic. When balanced, ideally the blue person supports

and organizes the violet person's ideas. When unbalanced, the blue person does not have confidence in the violet person's ideas. The blue person wants proof, facts, and numbers, and criticizes the violet person for being an unrealistic dreamer. If unbalanced, the violet person leads a disorganized life and engages in many frivolous private and business relationships. This behavior will irritate the organized blue partner.

RELATIONSHIPS VIOLET/INDIGO

This is an exciting and highly developed couple. They can be pure visionaries and pioneers. They both are interested in people and cultures and love to travel. They seek truth and a higher connection to the universe. They work for peace and the spiritual development of this planet. The violet person's strong leadership qualities and the indigo person's highly intuitive mind and belief-system have the potential of uniting in art and other forms of expression. The violet person's need to be the centre of attention does not have to compete with the subdued indigo personality. An unbalanced violet person tries to dominate an indigo partner. The indigo person does not understand this. If the situation becomes too annoying, the indigo person will leave the relationship. When balanced, each person gathers strength from the other. The indigo person gets all his/her questions answered. The violet person receives inspiration to do the things s/he needs to do.

Violet Interior Design

This colour is rarely used inside, except for beauty salons and theatres, in which both the walls and chairs are often in this colour. This colour energy gives inspiration and is spiritually uplifting. If too predominant in rooms used every day, violet can be very hard on the entire organism.

Violet Energy Drinks

Nervous states, mental conditions, and eye problems benefit from violet energy drinks. A glass every day would be of general benefit to the body.

Violet Gemstones

The main gemstone of violet people is the amethyst. Many people are strongly attracted to amethyst stones. They feel that the stone will help and guide them on the right spiritual path. Unfortunately, the amethyst does not hold its power for very long. But a new amethyst will come along in time as a new carrier of violet ray energy. In the meantime, the amethyst does its part by balancing feelings, thoughts, and the subconscious mind with the physical body.

Violet Foods
Violet food includes grapes, black currants, beets, eggplants, and purple broccoli.

The Violet Centre—Organs And Glands
The violet chakra is located at the top of the head. It is connected to the pineal gland. This gland is reactive to light. The violet centre connects us to the highest and most divine level, which is far beyond our area of understanding.

Affirmations For Violet People
"Today I need help from your great mental and spiritual strength. I need help to lift my thoughts to idealistic goals. I need the violet energy. I feel violet. I am violet."

Too Much Violet Energy–Overactive
Too much violet energy can result in spiritual revelations. Some people–artists and poets, for example can use this energy in their work. On the other hand, many other people cannot relate to this type of experience, which can create uneasiness and confusion.

Too Little Violet Energy–Underactive
This creates a feeling of inner emptiness and senselessness which can be overwhelming. Many people become very selfish and self-centred in their quest to fill this void. They misjudge and choose ideals that are not any good and then they are left disappointed or let down.

Answers from page 44.
1. Red 2. Orange 3. Yellow 4.Green 5. Blue 6. Indigo 7. Violet

Characteristics Of Violet People

Positive

Great mental strength
Inspirational leaders
Inspirational speakers
Inspirational artists
Inspirational teachers
Friendly
Fair
Humanistic
Self-sacrificing
Spiritually developed
Charismatic
Creative in every way
Artistic in every way
Charming
Ability to wonder
  and see the
mystical things in life
Ability to transform
  and inspire others
Spiritually creative

Negative

Feels superior
+ Think they are
    better than others
+ Think they know
    better than others
+ Snobbish
+ Arrogant
+ Without faith
+ Fanatical
+ Black magic and
    the occult
+ Unfaithful
+ Calculating
+ Exhibitionist
+ Megalomaniac
+ Uncontrollable
    Daydreamer
+ Critical
  See themselves
    negatively
  Nymphomaniac
  Destructive

The Positive And Negative Qualities

I t is important that you learn how to use the properties of the colour energies correctly so that you can learn how to balance or actually get rid of certain unwanted qualities.

In Chapter 3, there is a section which lists the positive and negative characteristics of each colour. In the positive side of the column you will notice some of the traits are marked with a + sign which indicates that this quality is being used in an unbalanced or extreme manner. Consider, for example, the quality of sensitivity; this is a good quality to have, but if you are overly sensitive it is not good for you or others.

If there is a + symbol beside a characteristic on the negative side of the column, it means that you have *too much* of that particular colour energy. You can then reestablish balance by using the complementary colour of the colour the quality is listed under. So for example, in the green section there is a + sign by the characteristic greedy. This indicates that you have too much green energy and to balance yourself you should use the red energy. Give extra notice to where the +'s occur on the negative side, because that is where all excessive behaviour happens. If there is no + on the negative side, it means that the negativity is caused by having *too little* of that particular colour energy. You need to get more of that colour's energy in order to regain your balance.

It would be great if people could get rid of their qualities marked with a + sign on the negative side. Find a good positive colour quality you would like and concentrate on that quality. You have won a great battle if you can wipe the negative words off from your list.

There are many colour energies people can relate to; in fact you are made up of all the colours, but you may use some of the colours more than others. Perhaps there are some colours you would like to use more. You can take the test below to see if you recognize yourself on the positive or the negative side of the colour energies. If you answer 'yes' to a question A, you are on the positive side of the energy. If you answer 'yes' to question B, you are on the negative side. If you are on the negative side you should try to change to the positive side. Change is always easier if you have a system to work with. Using a T-account to find your strong and weak sides is a good start. The assignment below is a test to see if you are on the positive or negative side of a colour.

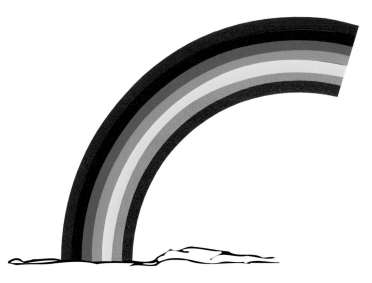

Red
❑ A. Do I finish the projects I start?
❑ B. Do I start too many projects? Do I outwear myself trying to finish them all? Do I become angry, irritated and aggressive when things are not going my way?

Orange
❑ A. Am I happy about all my friends and consider them a part of my "family"? Do I like to protect and serve my friends?
❑ B. Do I become frustrated and confused when I feel that I am not one hundred percent accepted for who I am?

Yellow
❑ A. Do I use my intellect to look for truth and justice in all situations?
❑ B. Do I use my intellect to criticize and judge others? Do I analyze and mistrust everything and everyone?

Green
☐ A. Do I love people and all living creatures without expecting love in return?
☐ B. Do I live in fear that everything I own will be taken from me and that the one I love will leave me?

Blue
☐ A. Have I managed to organize my life so that my work and my private life are in harmony? Do I feel that I am faithful and honest with myself?
☐ B. Do I rationalize everything so that I have lost contact with my emotions? Has my willpower made me blind to other life values?

Indigo
☐ A. Do I use my intuition properly so that I do what I have to learn on earth with insight and love?
☐ B. Do I dream and run away from reality? Has my life become too chaotic?

Violet
☐ A. Do I use my imagination and inspiration to produce positive and beneficial results? Do I affect other people positively and do I play a positive role in changing their outlook on reality?
☐ B. Do I let my fantasies and dreams control my life? Do I dream about things and inventions I will never realize? Do I let my frustrations over not getting things done convert into sexual passion?

AM I ONLY ONE COLOUR?

No, you are a rainbow of all the seven colours energies that flow from the sun to the earth. People, animals, plants, minerals, and water all receive energy from the sun's light. Think of yourself as a power plant which gathers water from various sources, then transforms the water into energy. This is what you do when the seven colour energies flow through you in energy pathways (also known as meridians); you just use some of these energy sources more than others in your daily life.

In Chapter 3 you read about the meaning and the power of the different colour energies. One day you might need another energy in addition to the one you use daily. There are several techniques to help you switch to another colour energy–I find bathing in colour the simplest way for me to fill up on the energy I need. The energy we need is available within all of us–we just have to learn how to use it. When someone is not using all the energy available, s/he is only working on "half power." This will create psychological and physical health problems. The many tasks we have to accomplish each day will seem heavy and difficult if we do not take advantage of all the energy available through our own inner "power plant."

What if we choose to "do it with colours?" We will then have to use our incredible brain power to help us figure out what we need.

> *For example, what if you need the red energy in your life? You need courage and willpower to make a decision, or to help you deal with a crisis in your life. You feel scared and insecure. You have little self-confidence. Basically, you do not have enough energy to solve your problems. At that point you decide to "do it with colours."*

Everybody can do it! It is up to you. Choose the colour energy you need. Look it up in Chapter 3 on the seven rainbow colours. Read about the positive and negative sides of the energy you want. Decide on a goal you want to achieve. Decide, choose the energy you need, and use it!

HOW CAN YOU LIVE IN BALANCE?

You have to know yourself. You must know who you are in order to live a balanced life. If you do not know yourself, you can learn about yourself. There are many colour tests to help you find out about yourself. There are also many knowledgeable people who work with colours and can explain what the colours represent. Max Lüscher, Marie Louise Lacy, and Karl Ryberg have developed tests based on choosing colour combinations. What colours you choose and in what order will tell you about yourself.

Colour Energy has a colour test available as well. Our test is based on 133 questions that you answer "yes," "sometimes," or "no" to. The questionnaire, in fact, is based on this book. When you figure out which colour is your main energy, you will be able to look back at the colour chapter and read if you are positively or negatively balanced.

Often one will be on the negative side because the energy centres do not have enough energy or the energy centres cannot access the energy properly. You can sometimes feel the negative side gaining more and more power and then against your own will you behave and react negatively. What do you do then? First find out if the negative reactions are caused by too little or too much energy. If you have too little energy you will have to add the specific colour energy. If you have too much, you will have to add the complementary colour energy, or use the colour that you feel will calm you down and get you in balance. Remember, nobody knows you better than yourself. It may sound complicated because you will have to check the pages that list the colour characteristics in order to find out how to balance yourself. But don't give up. It will pay off. You will learn the drill fast. Remember it is for your own good. When you know what you need to get in balance, you will start adjusting yourself.

How Do You Know Who You Are?

You know you are born.
You know your name.
You know what country you are from.
You may know who your parents or relatives are.
You know what you experienced and learned in life.
You know how you would like to present yourself in front of others and yourself.

But is this you? For most of us this is enough. Yet, sometimes you may wonder and think about the meaning of life. Or maybe there has been a dream, an incident, a play, a book or a music piece that touched you deep inside, but you don't know why that is. Something troubling hurts and feels tender in the heart region. You may feel pressure in your throat and head area, a feeling of discomfort, and a perception of "I can't handle this." That is when most people lose touch with their inner life. But some people ask themselves, "Is it an 'I' inside myself?" And it is. There is more than one "I" inside yourself. The "I" you know is the conscious, will-orientated and self-ruling "I". But you are so much more. You are body, soul, and

How Do You Know Who You Are?

mind. What you experience as the "I" in this trinity is your thoughts. What you feel when your feelings take form, is your soul's desperate fight to try and reach you. It is a conscious action when you accept that there is more than one "I" in you. When you acknowledge that to live consists of a teamwork of several "I's", you will then be able to work and live in harmony with your body and soul. And you will be able to live your life fully. You are then truly alive. To speak, to listen and to help your body like itself–is pure knowledge. You must understand love and have the willpower to let your body be happy. And you have to have knowledge of how your body works. Now, you know how to be yourself, but do you know exactly who you are?

Here is a little test to find out which you are using more of–body, feelings, or thoughts. Make three columns to correspond to the body, feelings, and thoughts.

BODY	FEELINGS	THOUGHTS

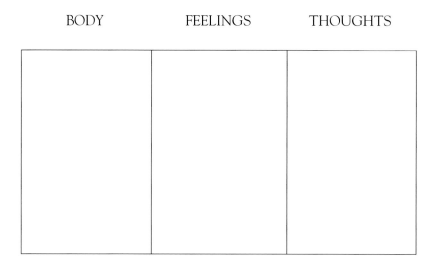

Try to fill up the columns with words that would describe yourself best. For example, "I walk a lot," "I like to work with my body," or "I think a lot," "I like to plan," etc. When you fill out these columns with words that describe yourself, which of these columns do you feel most at home in? Write down which one–body, feelings, or thoughts–you use the most.

Colour Energy Test
HOW YOU CAN USE
THE TEST PRACTICALLY

In the back of the book there is a test. You can fill it out after you read the following.

Answer the questions honestly and truthfully, and it will tell you what energy creates your personality. The test will tell you which colour is your main energy and your next six energies in their descending order. You use seven different energies as energy sources. Your body collects power from these seven energies. Your vitality, your attitude towards life, your experiences and insight begins with the seven energy sources. When you know what your resources are, you can then set your goals in life.

If you find out after taking the test that you use very little of the orange energy, it may mean that you are insecure and lack faith in yourself and your abilities. You do not use the energy that gives you confidence and independence. What can you do about this? Many things. You can start to look at how the orange colour presents itself in your surroundings. What kind of people use the orange colour in their clothing. How is orange used in commercials and interior design. Let's try an experiment with the colour. Take an orange *Colour Bath* and let your body and soul feel the orange energy.

The bottom line is, if you want to develop a specific energy you will have to work at it. You will have to be awake when the energy presents itself. For example, the indigo and violet are energies that are not earth bound. Indigo and violet are universal and inspired by God. These are the energies that help us to contact our inner worlds. These energies tell us that we are not only physical human beings, but we need a breath of spirit, a stream of inspiration, to lift us out of our earthly thinking and into our higher self. When this happens we will understand and appreciate the people who affect others by their actions. Think about Martin Luther King, Mother Theresa and many others, especially in the fields of art, literature, and music.

After you have taken the test you will be able to see from your own colour energy if the red energy is in balance. If you are uncertain you can look at your own T-

How You Can Use The Test Practically

account balance sheet to find out if you are on the positive or negative side of red. If the red energy is far out on the negative side, you will have to get it in balance. If you have too little energy, you will be lacking the courage, willpower to act. You are then lacking red energy. What do you do?

1) You acknowledge that you are not in balance.

2) You will select a tactic to correct the situation.

I suggest that you do this with colours. Make up your mind to take a red bath. Put yourself in a life-giving and energetic red bath. Feel how the physical and warm red energy fills your body. Feel the colour with all your senses. Open up to the energy and let your body utilize the power. Imagine that red blood is flowing in your veins, that you are breathing red flames, and that you shine with red energy. This is you today. Tomorrow you may need blue energy. What a colourful world you live in!

5

COLOUR ENERGY BATH WATER

Several years ago I attended a weekend seminar in which Peter Goldman from the White Lodge in England delivered an inspiring, eloquent, and humorous lecture on the philosophy of life. He gave us an introduction into the world of colours through the use of meditation. "Imagine," he said, " that you are sitting and that the colour orange is showering down upon you. You feel that you are having a bath in this refreshing colour." Usually, I have no difficulty visualizing things including colours. But I just could not visualize myself taking an imaginary colour shower. While I meditated with a hundred other people in this crowded and intense atmosphere a voice inside my head said, "You are going to make *Colour Bath*™." "Yes," I said to myself, and I went home with this wonderful idea As far as I knew, nobody else in the world had thought of coloured bath water before. It took me about two years before the idea of coloured bath water became reality. These were exciting and colourful years during which I took *Colour Baths* several times a day. It was very important to me that the baths had the right colour intensity and the right vibration. You would think that I would have become sick and tired of taking baths. On the contrary, I gained more and more energy and strength. Even now, I take at least one, sometimes two, *Colour Baths* a day.

WHY DID I DEVELOP *COLOUR BATH?*

I developed *Colour Bath* because I wanted to share with others the joy of getting to know oneself better. You will probably ask yourself, "Why do I have to take *Colour Baths* in order to get to know myself better?" You do not take a *Colour Bath* for the sole purpose of getting to know yourself better, but also to "recharge" yourself with the type of energy you need. It could be energy to rest, or to gain power, courage, creativity or faith. The *Colour Baths* will help you to find yourself. You can recharge yourself with the colour you need simply by bathing in the colour. For example, if you have lost contact with your feelings and emotions, you would use an orange, indigo, or green *Colour Bath*. Or if you have lost contact with your willpower, you would use red, yellow, blue, or violet. You would choose the colour best for you own situation. Once you learn about the qualities each colour represents, you will be able to choose the right colour for yourself. Believe in yourself, and you will choose the right colour. You get to know yourself, because every time you immerse yourself in a different colour you meet another aspect of yourself. Each colour represents a part of you–some of those parts you will recognize and acknowledge; other parts you may not recognize.

How To Make COLOUR BATH Work For You

After you have selected the type of energy you need, take the *Colour Bath* that represents that particular energy and put it in your bath water. For example, you might decide you need more physical energy and take a red bath. Unconsciously the body will be preparing for the bath. Messages from the brain will be going out informing the various parts of the body that the red energy is now being supplied. Your body is preparing itself to receive the red energy. Then you enter the tub. The coloured water surrounds you and embraces your naked body. Your eyes, skin, and consciousness now know that you are sitting in a red bath. Allow thoughts, impressions, experiences, and memories to run freely. Be open to all your senses and feelings. Just be there; be open to the sensations of being in the water. Be playful. Then, let your willpower convert thoughts into words. Get in touch with your subconscious mind by speaking out loud to yourself. Tell yourself what you want to achieve with the *Colour Bath* and why you need this particular colour energy. Your body and soul know exactly what energies you need–trust them.

This is all about energy. You needed one hundred percent of a particular colour, and on this particular day you chose red. After you get out of the bath, you will be charged with the clean red energy. All you need to do is dry yourself off and challenge the new day. Your body is prepared to give you the energy you need–just go out and use it!

Colours You Dislike

Let's talk about colours you do not like. See if you can recognize yourself in any of the following descriptions. Maybe your partner, child, or friends have said they don't like a particular colour; let's find out what it means.

Why Did I Develop COLOUR BATH?

RED

If you do not like red it might have something to do with your outlook on life. You may feel that life has been a big disappointment. Or maybe you are tired and lack vitality. Have you set your goals too high? It is not easy if you are ambitious and things do not work out as planned. Remember that success cannot be measured in dollars only. You might also be sexually frustrated. If you are a man you might fear impotence.

ORANGE

If you do not like orange, you might have a problem dealing with your emotions. Without orange energy, life can become joyless and depressing. Feelings of happiness and openness become blocked. You feel lonely and you have no social life. You might also feel jealous and irritated by people who live an easy, worry-free life. Your sex urge is gone and you avoid any social contact.

YELLOW

The spark of life must have left you if you do not like yellow. Your wishes and your hopes must have been shattered. You feel left out of life. If you feel like this you should seek assistance right away. You also oppose anything that is new or based on the intellect. You might be critical of any new research or new age or esoteric philosophies.

GREEN

If you do not like green you probably feel that nobody understands you or appreciates you for who you are. There is definitely something amiss when the colour representing balance, nature, and peace is disliked. You might become a lonely hermit, withdrawing from people, because you are jealous of their sense of security and safety. Your will to live has become subdued, and you blame others and your life situation. You feel that the world has turned against you and that you are a victim of the world's injustice.

BLUE

You most likely have suffered a personal loss or a failed relationship if you do not like blue. You might feel that others have had better opportunities than you. They have been lucky while you have been unlucky and unsuccessful. Or maybe you feel guilty, because you wasted too many years trying to become successful. Usually everybody likes blue. It is almost unnatural to not like blue. If you dislike blue, you should ask yourself these questions: "Why do I hate blue? Am I bored? Does my life lack excitement? Do I need a change of scenery? Am I sexually frustrated? Am I a lazy person or have I managed to convince myself that I am worthless? Is there no chance for me? Have my emotions left me?"

INDIGO

You are not the only person in the world who does not like any shade of this colour, from a dark indigo to lavender-blue. Indigo is not often used in interior design or for clothing. If you do not like this colour it means that you do not like whatever is different or what you do not understand. You measure everybody according to your own standards, perceptions, and goals. Do you feel inadequate? Do you feel that you lack education, intelligence, charm, or humour? Do you feel wrongly treated by others? Do you judge others before you know their background and circumstances?

VIOLET

 If you do not like violet, you may feel that people try to force their opinions, faith, religious views, and will upon you. You feel overpowered by others. You feel they want to control what you feel and do. You feel people trample over your integrity and self-worth. Do you feel a lack of inspiration in your daily life?

COLOURS AND PRAYER

What is prayer other than a conversation between yourself and God? To pray you fold your hands and express your wishes with a pure and focused mind. You usually use one, two, or three different types of energy in praying. First, you open up your heart chakra to let the green energy flow. Next, consciously or unconsciously, your intuitive indigo energy plays a part in helping to connect to a higher power. Lastly, the blue energy helps you to formulate the words of the prayer and to put them into conscious thought. You pray when you use concentration and willpower to ask for help from your heart. This cleanses the soul, and connects you to the transcendent energy of God. If you get an answer then you will feel the violet energy.

COLOURS AND AFFIRMATIONS

An affirmation, directly translated, means a confirmation. So when we repeat an "affirmation" we confirm again and again what we wish or ask for. When I sit in my colour energy bath I wish to achieve something. I have chosen a colour for the energy I need that particular day. I will repeat loudly, again and again, what it is I wish to have. I use a red affirmation for a red energy, a blue affirmation for blue energy, etc. You can make your own affirmation according to your own needs. Or use affirmations from other sources. The affirmations that I have formulated and use are listed with each colour under Affirmations in Chapter 3.

HOW DOES
COLOUR BATH REALLY WORK?

Assignment:

After you have read the chapter on the different colours, you can test yourself with this simple assignment. Prepare seven T-accounts, one for each colour. Under the appropriate colour T- account, using the list in Chapter 3, write your positive and negative qualities. When that is done you will quickly be able to see which colour accounts balance and which do not. You will also be able to see which colour dominates your personality, according to the length of your colour account lists. If you have got, for example, 20 positive and negative qualities in the red, 15 in the yellow, and just 4 in the indigo, it will be easy to see that red is a dominating energy in your life. A good idea is to give points to each colour. In this case red will receive 20 points, yellow 15, and indigo 4, etc. An important detail to remember is that both the negative and positive sides of the T-account determine the amount of energy you use of a particular colour. In the T-account, if the negative side weighs more that the positive side, it means that you receive plenty of that colour's energy, but you are just using it in the wrong way. Remember, if you have negative side you also have a positive side. What it all boils down to is maintaining a balance.

As *Colour Bath* has been in use for several years now, we have gathered a large amount of information on how *Colour Bath* works. Many people are very open towards colours and get results immediately, while others are very skeptical, but nevertheless curious. I would like to share a story of one such curious and skeptical person.

Randi, a law school student, attended one of Colour Energy's courses. Randi's main colour was yellow, and her indigo energy was way out of balance. She seemed very gloomy, depressed, and detached from her life. It was obvious that she was on the negative side of herself. After the course ended, we stayed in contact with Randi. According to Randi's own account, this is what happened to her. Randi started taking red and orange baths, at first very unwillingly. She did not believe that taking a bath in colour could change anything. But she felt a difference after each bath. As she said, "I had no idea that I could become addicted to red baths." Randi decided not to continue with her law studies, but to work with colours and light. She went to the United States to attend a course on how light affects people. Randi attended more Colour Energy courses as well. Today she looks ten years younger, and is full of positive and life-embracing energy. In fact she challenges life.

Numerous people have taken Colour Energy courses and have started to use colours to change their lives. They have exciting stories to tell about how colours have affected them.

One special account is about two sisters, Rose and Vigdis and their uncompromising willingness to help their father who was seriously ill with pancreatic cancer. This story is not about healing an illness but about how colours can strengthen the will and improve the quality of life. The doctors had given up hope, and the father was despondent and apathetic. Rose and Vigdis could not accept this and turned to colours for help. First of all, they got a private room for their father and began to change the room to a sunny paradise. The used yellow bed linens and curtains. The room was decorated with yellow and orange flowers. They gave their father yellow food and drinks, such as bananas and lemonade. They dressed themselves in yellow, orange and red to stimulate their father's spark for life. From a tape we use in our meditation classes, they played music that opens the yellow solar plexus chakra. Furthermore, they got a crystal and gemstone expert to help them place yellow gemstones and crystals charged with positive power on their father's body. You are probably asking yourself, "Why all that yellow?" It is because yellow is the colour that stimulates the pancreas, and a gland that lacks energy needs to be stimulated.

Of course all this created enormous attention at the hospital and all the nurses had to have a peek into the "yellow room." Happily, all the work to make their father feel better paid off. Their father's health started to improve. He began eating better. He started to read the newspaper and to regain his cheerfulness. Meanwhile, the sisters had heard about an immune building program for cancer called the "Nitter-treatment." They began using this treatment and also homeopathic medicine.

How Does COLOUR BATH Really Work?

This story is unique because the two sisters had the courage and strength to change the hospital system in order to carry out the colour treatment. They did all this work with colours to help their father regain his joy for life, and to give him encouragement and strength to deal with his illness. Their father died several months later, happy. Their efforts had not been in vain. As Rose explained, "On the day dad died, he said 'I have had such a fantastic summer that I am ready to let go. I am not afraid anymore.'"

Paal is another example of how colour can balance the positive and negative energy qualities. Paal, in fact, went on television to tell about his experience with colours.

Paal was a young and creative hotel manger with a very demanding job. There was very little time for Paal to relax and to express his emotional or creative side. Paal was totally stressed out from working eighteen hour days. One afternoon, he took an orange bath to gain more energy. What happened? He slept for sixteen hours. This happened because Paal needed to balance the energies in his life. In fact we all need to find that balance between our emotional and willpower energies. It is important that the life-promoting and impulsive emotional energies have a say in our lives. Willpower and responsibility can easily knock over and paralyze the more sensitive feelings. Paal regained a balance in his life after several orange baths.

We are very careful about the information that is let out to the media on colour healing. We believe it is up to the scientists, doctors, and alternative healers to meet the challenge of finding out how colours affect people health-wise. What we want to do is tell about the energy available for us through colours. We also wish to inform interested people about how they can gain knowledge of themselves and others. But every week we hear a new story on how colour has helped someone. We have started to categorize these incidents to gain more insight into the power of colour. Predictably most cases are psychosomatic. I believe that most illnesses are caused by something quite different than what they are being treated for.

Mona is a patient of a therapist who has participated in courses offered by Colour Energy. Mona suffered from severe asthma attacks and was often hospitalized. Her therapist recommended that Mona try an orange bath to help her asthma. One day Mona suffered a severe asthma attack and in desperation she decided to try an orange bath. At first her breathing problems became worse, but then everything calmed down. When she stepped out of the bath her attack was over. She has tried this several times and now believes that orange baths are an excellent way of averting attacks.

Orange energy is incredibly effective. Most people have a poor relationship with the colour orange. They do not like the colour. Or perhaps they think that orange does not suit them. Some people do not think orange is a good colour for home decor. But the colour orange is the elixir of life. It reminds me of childhood, and of carefree days of happiness and laughter. Orange colour is about being oneself, about letting go of fear, and about just being alive.

A lot of adults and children have problems sleeping. A warm bath would help, but a *Colour Bath* will have a much more beneficial effect. We always recommend indigo and blue baths for children with sleeping problems. For children with lively imaginations and who have nightmares, a blue bath would be best. If they only have lively imaginations, then they should use a weak indigo bath.

> *An amusing story is about a one and half year old boy named Christian. Christian never had any problems sleeping. But one evening his mother, who had read a lot about the meanings of colours, gave him an orange bath. Christian had fun in the bath. But after the bath, both Christian and his mother were unable to sleep. Christian wanted to play and be silly, and the mother was equally energetic. The mother learned an important lesson. No orange baths before bedtime!*

Bed linens and clothing can have a big influence on children. This is probably something we do not think about at all.

> *A mother contacted us and explained that her child, Kari, was noisy, wild, and hyper-active. Kari had restless sleeps, and some nights she did not sleep much at all. The mother had heard about Colour Energy on a radio program, and was wondering if colours could help Kari. We talked with the mother for quite awhile. We found out that Kari usually wore red clothes and that she had red bed linens and curtains in her bedroom. We told the mother to change the colour of the bedroom to blue, and to dress Kari in only blue and green coloured clothing. We usually hear back from the people we help, and indeed we did this time as well. Kari's mother phoned and told us Kari had slept one night in her new blue bedroom, and that she was like a new little person the next morning.*

When it became known that we were working with a personality test, a lot of psychologists and others who work directly with people came to see us. They were curious. Some were open and some were skeptical. For me, the most important thing is for people to be curious, as that is the biggest drive toward progress.

I would like to tell you about Per, a man in his fifties, who, in his capacity as a teacher in the retraining field, had taught many courses. He considered himself to be a person who had a lot of extra energy, but one who worked out of happiness and enthusiasm. We did the colour test before he told us what his profession was. We found that Per's main colour was blue, with yellow and red following closely behind. After having talked to him about the meaning of the colours, and the effect of the energy being on the negative side, he came to realize that he had little contact with his emotional energies, especially the indigo and orange. He told us, "Now I see why I don't always get everybody involved during my courses. It is as if we do not understand each other. Now I know what I can do about it."

There you go. Often it only takes a few things to fall into place and you understand things better. A researcher and part-time psychologist took our colour test, and told us afterwards that of all the personality tests he had taken for employment counseling and personal development, he thought our system was the easiest to use and understand. He felt that our colour test provided a positive avenue for people to change and grow. Now if he wanted to change something about himself, he knew how.

This reminds me of a couple who took our colour test. They had heard about Colour Energy through a radio program in which we talked about colours for the home and for interior decor. They took the colour test so we could find out which colours they had in common, and which colours they needed for themselves personally. In a home that is shared, it is very important to choose colours that harmonize with the couple's need for rest and stimulation. The couple, Kari and Petter, were both resourceful personalities, but very different. Petter was a man who was very strong-willed. His highest ranking colours were blue, yellow, and violet. Kari was a very emotional person with the colours yellow, green, and orange dominating. They were both on their negative sides, and probably had been for many years. Their children were adults and had moved out. But instead of growing together, Kari and Petter had grown apart. They both blamed each other for their problems. They criticized and neglected each other on a daily basis. We were puzzled as to why they had come to see us about colours for their home, when their marriage was hanging by a thin thread. Two of our therapists spent five hours working with them in turns. We were working with a couple who did not understand each other. We had to tell Kari how Petter felt, how he perceived things, and what he needed. Petter was a systematic, a logical thinker, and a person who needed his own room to think in. Petter had to analyze and think before making a decision. Kari was directly the opposite–impulsive, creative, quick to act, and outgoing. Kari was warm with a big need for contact. When Kari needed contact, Petter became withdrawn. Kari then became hurt, and blamed Petter for this. And Petter, because of his strong blue energy, could not have sex when there were unresolved issues. On the other hand, the emotionally dominated Kari would forget all conflicts and want to have sex. You can see there was a bit more work involved here than just decorating a new house.

Of course you cannot change in five hours. But you can gain insight into problems and begin to see things from a different perspective. If you want to you can eventually change. Kari and Petter's assignment was to concentrate on finding their own balance, and then to learn how the other thinks and relates to things. The most important ingredient in any relationship is respect. You have to understand that your partner should not have to change their personality, but be helped to regain a balance on their positive side. Petter has kept in touch with *Colour Energy*. He told us that they have become deeply involved with colours. They are using colours to learn to understand themselves and their relationship. Petter said, "What I need Kari has, and what Kari does not have I have." So actually they are perfect for each other. They can fulfill each other and learn from one another. Imagine how exciting it must be to live in a relationship with such challenges.

FREQUENTLY ASKED QUESTIONS ABOUT *COLOUR BATH*

You probably have many questions. How long do I have to stay in the bath? How often should I use *Colour Bath*? How much colour should I add to the bath water? Can children use *Colour Bath*?

Stay in the bath for as long as you feel comfortable. Sometimes a quick bath will be sufficient and other times you might lie there for half an hour and still not feel you have had enough time–that is what is so wonderful about *Colour Bath*. However, if you are ill, you should watch how long you stay in the tub. Remember that a warm bath is good when you are tired and want to sleep. A cooler bath is stimulating and energy giving. The frequency of the baths will depend on whether you are using *Colour Bath* for treatment purposes, or if you are just taking baths for pleasure. I have taken *Colour Baths* for years now and I usually bathe every day. Depending on the situation, I use *Colour Bath* to help me relax or to get energy. I use the energy of colours consciously in my daily life. I often wake up in the morning with a totally different energy than the one I intended to use. Every morning, before I get out of bed, I go through my plans for the day. I analyze my day to find out which colour energy I will need to carry out my plans. When all that is done, it is time for my morning bath in the colour I need energy from. Sometimes in the evening, when I am going out to a party, I take an orange bath to re-energize myself. Then I will be sure to have a great time.

The strength of the colour depends on the size of your bathtub and how strong you want the colour. For example, if you have a bottle of the red *Colour Bath* and you want to take a soft rose bath, all you have to do is add the colour directly to the bath water until you get the desired shade. This way of producing pastel shades is the same with all the colours. Pastel violet is truly beautiful. It is like bathing in an amethyst crystal. We recommend that you use pastel shades of red, indigo and violet for young children. A weak lavender/indigo *Colour Bath* is good for restless children with sleeping problems. Rose is a beautiful colour for children any time. Pastel violet is wonderful for disheartened and unmotivated children. Children can use blue, green, yellow and orange *Colour Bath* at full strength. Although blue can be effective in helping children sleep, it also can be a mental stimulant to improve a child's reading, writing, and speaking abilities. Red, orange, yellow, and violet are not evening bath colours as they are stimulating and rejuvenating.

What if you do not have a bathtub? No problem, take a footbath so you can sit and look at the colours, or borrow a family member's or a friend's bathtub. There is always a way if you really want to colour bathe.

> *Tom told us great story of someone who benefited from footbaths. Tom's 72 year old grandmother had poor circulation that really affected her legs. She could hardly walk. Her doctor recommended diuretic medicine and told her to learn to live with the pain. Tom recommended green Colour Bath to his grandmother. She started taking green footbaths every morning and evening. She was truly*

amazed when the swelling went down and she could use her old shoes again. Her amazement increased when she had to go out and buy shoes two sizes smaller to even have something to wear. She became more cheerful and high spirited and is now a staunch supporter of green Colour Bath.

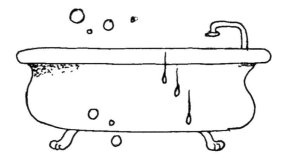

6

THE EFFECT OF COLOUR

Auras

What is an aura? The aura consists of various electromagnetic energies of different strengths, which surround the physical human body as beams. All that is alive has electromagnetic radiation; even stones give out vibrations and radiation, but human beings have the strongest and most illuminating electromagnetic energy. Cemyon Kirlian, from Russia, developed a photographic technique now known as Kirlian photography, that shows the electromagnetic radiation of people and plants. Walter Kilner also researched the aura in a laboratory setting. He observed that a healthy body radiated clear colours such as red, yellow, and blue, while illnesses appeared as misty, muddy, grey tones. There are few people today who would dispute that everyone is surrounded by an electromagnetic field.

Auras vary from person to person, and an individual's aura changes all the time. The emotional body changes quickly, while the mental body is more stable. These fluctuations occur because the aura responds to our constantly changing thoughts and feelings. If you are depressed your aura will be misty; when you are happy the colours will be clear. Imagine what a sight it is for people who can see the seven layers of the aura, each with its own vibration and purpose. There are many books and courses available to help you understand and "see" auras. For those who are interested, here is an explanation of the seven auric bodies that form seven different layers around the physical body. Each layer is also connected to a chakra.

The seven layers are:

1) The etheric body. Etheric comes from the word ether, and means a condition between energy and matter.
2) The emotional body.
3) The thought body.
4) The astral body.
5) The etheric template body.
6) The celestial body. It means super mundane.
7) The Ketheric template, or causal body. This means the cause body.

The First Invisible Body Layer—The Etheric Body

The etheric body carries, receives, stores, and transfers the energy that surrounds us all the time. This level of energy is mostly concerned with physical healing. It is here that illness first starts to manifest itself. It is through the etheric body or health-aura that we can stay healthy. Fresh air, natural surroundings, and positive thoughts are also important in keeping healthy. We can even cure ourselves if we can stay away from negative people and places. By this I mean people who purposely choose to use negative energy to affect others. Remember that the amount of energy in positive and negative qualities is the same. Places that might be considered negatively charged include houses where people have used energy negatively or where a crime has taken place. These two things will draw energy from you. It is important to think about this when you are ill. The etheric body works to remove the psychic and psychological toxins, just as the kidneys remove poison from the blood. If the body is weak and does not have enough power to keep the negative energies out, you will end up with a psychosomatic symptom. The physical body must then try to keep a balance or the symptom will turn into a true illness. The etheric body appears as a yellow/white layer. It pulsates and moves in a flowing motion.

The Second Invisible Body Layer—The Emotional Body

This body is associated with feelings. It circles the outer fringes of the physical body, and it flows more freely than the etheric body. It looks like a coloured cloud, made-up of a finer substance than the etheric body, flowing about five to seven centimetres away from the body. The emotional body contains all the brilliant, radiant colours of the rainbow.

The Third Invisible Body Layer—The Mental Body

This body is composed of even finer substances and it is associated with thoughts and mental processes. Usually it is seen as a translucent layer with a yellowish shimmer. The layer becomes bigger and clearer when the "owner" is busy concentrating on solving "problems." It is about eight to twenty centimetres away from the physical body. The mental body is also a structured body. Within the area of the mental body you can often see thought forms which appear as bubbles of different sizes and light.

The Fourth Invisible Body Layer—The Astral Body

The astral body has no definite form. It looks like different, beautifully coloured clouds which are much more beautiful than those of the emotional body. It has the same colours of the emotional body, but one colour has been added–rose–which stands for love. It is about fifteen to thirty centimetres from the body. The heart chakra of a loving and good person is full of rose light on the astral level. When two people fall in love you can see beautiful rose patterns flowing between their hearts. A stream of rose colour is also added to the always pulsating aura around the person. When people connect with each other, a tie grows out from a chakra to link them. These ties exist at all levels in the auric bodies. The deeper the connection, the longer and stronger the ties. When the connection is broken, the ties break as well and that can hurt. Big bubbles of colours in different shapes exist between people. Some are happy and good; others are unpleasant. You can often recognize the ties between people. At a party it is easy to see if there is any sexual connection between a man and a woman. There is communication at a level you can feel and sense, but cannot see.

The Fifth Invisible Body Layer—The Etheric Template Body

This is a copy of the etheric body, but it is around thirty to sixty centimetres away from the physical body. The "etheric template" works on keeping the etheric body in its original form if you fall ill and the etheric body becomes diffused. The most effective way to promote healing in this case is by sound. The etheric template body is seen as an almost transparent layer overtop a cobalt blue background.

The Sixth Invisible Body Layer—The Celestial Or Super Mundane Body

This is the emotional level of the spiritual plane. This layer is about sixty to eighty centimetres away from the physical body. At this layer we can feel spiritual ecstasy.

We can reach this level through meditation. Unconditional love floats between an open heart chakra and the celestial body. The celestial body has a nice vibrating light that is seen mostly in pastel colours. It is of a gold and silver, almost opaline nature. It looks like the beams around a candlelight.

The Seventh Invisible Body Layer—The Ketheric Template Or Causal Body (THE CAUSAL BODY MEANING THE CAUSE BODY)

This is the mental level of the spiritual plane. This layer is about seventy to ninety centimetres outside our physical body. When we bring our consciousness out to the seventh body we are close to the origin. At this level everything looks like colour vibrations. The causal body pulsates so quickly that it looks more like thousands of golden threads. At this layer a human being would look more like an egg having an outer shell not thicker than one centimetre. The outer shell is strong, the strongest of all the levels. Outside the egg a lot of ties are connected to the egg in different places. These ties originate from past lives. Ties coming from the head and throat are occurrences from your last life which you should learn more about in this life. Beyond the egg there is a cosmic level which we cannot understand with our limited experience.

WHO CAN SEE THE AURA?

We all had so-called "psychic abilities" when we were children and could see auras, but these talents are not considered normal, so we lose this ability to see as we grow older. People with an enormous indigo influence will of course "see" more than others, but with practice, anyone can see the auras that surround all living creatures.

Aura Photographs

Nowadays, special photographic systems exist that can photograph electro-magnetic energy. You can get a portrait of yourself in which you can see your aura with its different colours. The aura is not constant so the picture will change according to the changes in your feelings and thought patterns. It can be quite a pretty picture when the rainbow colours shine around you like a halo. Special cameras exist that can video tape your changing aura. You are able to see how the colours change in your aura when your thought patterns change. It is like looking at the Aurora Borealis.

Colour Energy in Norway has an Aura Vision camera that we use for doing colour personality analysis, either by itself or with our other colour tests. We think this development of aura photography is very exciting, and that in the future it will help to greatly increase our knowledge of aura medicine. It might be possible in the future to heal ourselves with thoughts long before we get any physical illness. We hope that aura pictures and aura diagrams will become accessible everywhere soon.

Precious Gemstones And Crystals

A lot of people have chosen to work with gemstones and crystals because of their beauty, and because they wish to spread positive energy. Gemstones and jewels have been used since ancient times, mostly for healing and protection purposes. Royalty and the clergy have always worn precious stones, not just for the beauty and richness they represented, but also for their protecting and giving qualities. Precious stones are concentrated energy of cosmic force and colour, and they generously radiate the special qualities of their clear, clean colour. The different waves and vibrational frequencies of these rays of colour affect people. We can draw on a gemstone's energy without it ever losing its power. Actually, if we use our gemstones with care and love, more brightness and energy will be added to them. Colours and brightness can be increased concurrently with our own energy and the colour energy we use. There is a constant interplay between us and the colour energies in the universe. Remember you have to learn to use a gemstone, just as you have to learn to use anything else. You can wear a piece of jewellery with a ruby in it, but you cannot make use of the ruby's power until you open yourself to the power that the ruby has. It is the same way with the colour energies, and with all other things you want to learn from. You have to open yourself up for the message. If you do not, there will always be an invisible door between you and the energies. Many people use crystals for meditation, or they carry a rose quartz in their pockets. Crystals and the users of crystals belong to the "New Age." Even though crystals were used long ago for religious and healing purposes, it still is the people of our time, the age of Aquarius, who are the moving power behind the great interest in crystals that exists today. It is a world full of power and beauty, and whoever wants to learn about the use of crystals for healing or well-being enters an exciting realm. There are many well-informed teachers and good books around to teach us about crystals. Put a clear quartz crystal in a glass of water. This will help balance the crystal formation in the water, and when you drink the water it will help you to a clearer consciousness. If you have a blocked chakra, lie down flat and place the stone that corresponds to that chakra (for example the carnelian gemstone corresponds to the spleen chakra) on that particular chakra spot.

Coloured Glass

Coloured glass is a common sight for our eyes nowadays, but it can also be a great experience for our taste buds. It is a feast for the eye and the palate to drink from coloured glass. Here is our recipe for "sun-kissed" water. Hopefully you can acquire glasses in all the different colours of the rainbow. Use a glass that is the same colour you need energy from. Fill the glass with clean water, and place the glass in the sunlight. Do not put the glass behind a window. Leave it in the sun for a couple of hours. The sun's beams will hit the coloured glass and energize the water with the colour energy you have chosen. If you drink one glass of each colour every day it would be like taking a multivitamin. For example, the red colour energy has it's own minerals such as iron. You will receive all the colours and the minerals they have, plus a dose of ultra violet energy. "Sun-kissed water" is stimulating for the whole organism and symbolically it affirms that the colour you have chosen is a needed energy.

Astrology

Remember that the sun is a star. Most people know or understand that the sun, moon, weather, and seasons influence us. It has been proven that all the planets, including the Earth, have an effect on the sun. These planets are closer to us than to the sun, so there is reason to believe that they affect the Earth as well. It is then easy to understand how the planets have a great influence on our bodies especially through the indigo chakra since our auric body has more of a connection to the universe than the physical body.

The Planets And The Seven Chakras

MUDLADHARA—RED
>Mars. The reproductive system.

SVADHISTANA—ORANGE
>Mercury. Kidney and hormonal system.

MANIPURA—YELLOW
>The Sun. The intestines.

ANAHATA—GREEN
>Venus. Love from the heart. All feelings

VISHUDDHA—BLUE
>Jupiter. Hearing and communication.

AJNA—INDIGO
>Saturn. Concentration, meditation, inner sight, psychic powers.

SAHASRARA—VIOLET
>Uranus. Turns all energies into white light.

Most people are concerned with sex, food, and survival. These needs are connected to the planets Mars, Mercury, and the Sun. When the planet Mars influences the red centre negatively, the raw sex energy will show up as a dark red aura. In that case it would be very helpful to know that the green energy from Venus can balance that. When sexual energy builds up inside people, it is very important that it does not come out in a negative way, which could result in violence and perversity. It is especially important that a red person releases her/his energy in a positive way. All in all, it is important that you understand who you are, why you are that way, and what can balance you.

Music

Every chakra energy centre has a tone and a sound that it is directly connected to. You probably have experienced getting goose bumps from certain music you like. Or maybe the music made you cry, and you had the feeling of belonging to something, being one with something. This feeling is connected to the tone that is yours. Special sounds in the form of monotonous vocal sounds can connect the sound to the cosmic sounds. This adds more consciousness to the centre. One of the sounds is "AOM." You can enhance every chakra by using sounds that will stimulate and open that particular chakra.

The red and the orange centres are connected to the letter U. The yellow centre has the letter AA. The green has A. Blue has I, and indigo and violet AI. Nowadays, you can find many special music pieces composed to stimulate the chakra centres. *Colour Energy* uses music composed by Norwegian Morten Alexander Joramo. This music was composed over six tones and has different beats that resonate with each chakra directly. We use this tape to enhance chakra-meditations.

Interior Design

Here are three questions you can ask yourself if you are about to redecorate, as colour choice is a very important consideration. Let all the members of your family answer the same questions. You will be surprised to see how many choose the same colours as yourself.

A. Which colour makes you happy and satisfied?
    (Close you eyes and try to feel the colour that comes to your mind.)
B. Which colour gives you strength and vitality?
    (What colour do you feel yourself receiving strength from?)
C. Which colour makes you feel safe, pleased, and secure?
    (Imagine the colour that gives you this feeling.)

A Few Colour Suggestions:

1. Vibrant strong colours like red, yellow, and bright blue make a room smaller.
2. Bright colours and all pastel colours make a room seem lighter and bigger. These colours are ideal for use in small rooms. Pastel colours are calm and relaxing.
3. White is used a lot in most homes. But too much white will make your house seem too cold. You can bring out a personal and airy atmosphere by adding a touch of your favourite colour.
4. Warm colours such as red, yellow, and orange combined with wooden furniture give a warm atmosphere. Cool colours like blue and indigo can almost make the temperature drop. Cool colours in your home make you dress warmer.

The Effect Of Colour

A small hint would be to use sixty-five percent of you favourite colour for walls and ceilings. Use the colour in all shades. Use twenty-five percent of your second colour choice for curtains and furniture. Use all colour shades here as well. You can use a third colour for the last ten percent on paintings and ornaments. You should compromise if several people have a say about the same room. Perhaps each person could decorate one room in the colours s/he likes.

It is important to separate your private home from your work place. A lot of people make their office cozy and comfortable like their homes. But too much colour or overly comfortable surroundings can reduce the concentration you need to do your job. It is very important to have the right colours in your place of business. White walls and walls with strong contrasts would be very tiring to look at constantly. A wall painted in strong dark blue will create a chaotic atmosphere. A wall that has a big window should not be painted with sharp colours. It would be much better to decorate the wall on the opposite side this way. Cool colours such as blue, green, or turquoise are best for offices and areas that need quiet and orderliness. These colours are also suitable for offices where people are dealing with finances or planning projects. They are less distracting and enhance concentration.

Warm colours, such as orange and green, are tremendously effective in places like bakeries, restaurants, and toy stores. Yellow would be very suitable for a bookstore or a library. Basically, you have to think about what you want out of the rooms before you paint or decorate the work place. Should the colour energy be focused on the company's clients or customers, or should it be aimed at those who work there? What kind of people do you work with? How can you stimulate them to perform and thrive better? Maybe the finance department should be painted one colour, and the creative sales department another colour. At home there are actually more things to consider as you probably will have several different personalities gathered under one roof. You should try to consider everybody when you paint or decorate your home. It can in fact be quite harmful to have an interior decorator come in and choose colours according to what is "in." Currently it is very popular to decorate with strong colours in every room. This can be extremely stimulating for one person, but very depressing and irritating for someone else. Do not forget that certain colours can make some children become restless or make it hard for them to concentrate. No, colours are not just for pleasure. Again, it all boils down to balance—too much or too little of certain colour energies.

The room that needs the most attention is the bathroom. The ancient Greeks and Romans knew that you gained strength by resting in a bath. Their baths were big and beautifully decorated. Nowadays baths have become smaller and smaller.

The Effect Of Colour

Often there is only a shower. Your day usually starts in the bathroom and that is why it is so important to paint this room in colours that will give you happiness. You should turn your bathroom into the place in your home where you draw strength and where your body finds peace and quiet. Lying in a bathtub feels wonderful and is pure luxury for the body and the soul. It is beneficial to spoil that part of yourself as well. Decorate and turn your bathroom into a restful place of refuge.

Some examples of colours to decorate you bathroom in:

> ROMANTIC: *All rose colours*
> SENSUAL: *Wine colours or burgundy*
> ENHANCES FEELINGS: *Peach, apricot, and salmon red*
> HAPPINESS: *Yellow, honey yellow, and sun yellow*
> CLARITY: *Turquoise, light blue, and azure*
> REFRESHING AND GOOD FOR HEALTH: *Green, forest green, or emerald*
> RELAXING: *Sea green and mint green*
> PEACEFUL: *Blue/green and ocean blue*

Clothes

> *"When she entered, the room became so much lighter and happier. She wore a bright poppy-red dress and seemed to radiate happiness and an appetite for life. He hurried towards her."*

There you go–this is how one colour can work. We affect each other and ourselves with the colours we wear. Imagine that you are going to visit a friend in the hospital who is recovering from heart surgery. Would you wear a bright red shirt or pants? You might have thought that the colour red would brighten up her/his day. But I do not think your friend would need red for that reason. Red would increase the blood flow and make the blood run faster. A green, blue, white, or yellow colour would be better. Or, yes, even orange. On the other hand if you are visiting a patient with a nervous disorder, do not use yellow. It can be an irritating energy for bad nerves.

What clothes should you wear when looking for a job? You should think about this carefully. If you are applying for a job in a bank, wear blue. The colour blue gives an impression of efficiency, order, and peace. You will project an image of intelligence and self control. If you are applying for a job in a creative environment wear indigo, orange, or violet. These are positive, outgoing, and inquisitive energies.

The Effect Of Colour

Yellow will inspire confidence when you are looking for a job as a teacher or librarian. Yellow is the colour of knowledge. You signal who you are with colours. And if you know the language of colours (chromolingua), your personality will be recognized through the clothes you wear and the colours you represent yourself with.

Imagine that you wake up one day feeling gloomy and a bit sad. It is not a day to conquer the world. What do you do? You probably will go to your closet and start going through your clothes. You will probably think, "No, I just cannot wear red today and not yellow either." Then you might end up wearing black, gray, brown, or something that is very neutral. Stop and think for a second! Why do you feel so down? Why do you not feel like conquering the world? Why does this day feel so wrong? Try to find the reason you feel so depressed. And try to find out what you really wish to accomplish that day. Then go to your closet and see if you have a suit in the colour that will help you with your day. You are looking for the energy that will help you with the activities you planned for the day. If you are using a lot of black, gray, and brown, remember that these are not colours. They do not give out any energy, and they do not receive energy either. Clothes give out signals and inspire you to do things, especially they are the right colour. Colours go in and out of fashion so that clothing manufacturers can entice people to buy a new wardrobe twice a year. But I do not think people are that easy to manipulate–nobody will wear alpine green or earth brown when they wish to wear yellow or red!

Fashion is not totally bad. It has done some good. Thanks to the fashion hunt for new colour combinations twice a year, we have gotten rid of the idea that yellow and violet do not go well together, or that orange is not a nice colour. The fashion dynasties have managed to break down colour complexes. All colours are okay to wear today, but not all colours feel comfortable. Since we wear clothes day and night, it is important that we emit the right colour impulses to our susceptible and sensitive skin surfaces. By the way, did you know that a certain yellow/green can cleanse the skin.

You can use colours consciously, especially through the clothes you wear. Make your own list on why you use this or that colour. A colour might be very special to you, but perhaps the colour means something else to others. Try to find out why you like a colour. It will be understandable of course, if you say that you like a shade of blue because it matches your eye colour exactly. But there probably will be another reason why you are attracted to that particular colour as well. Try to find out. It will be exciting to find out more about yourself. Ask yourself, "Why do I like this colour and why do I not want to wear anything of that colour?" Clothing combinations often have a much bigger effect on others than the person wearing the clothes. Therefore, it is important to learn about colour combinations and their effects. Will the colour attract or repel? Will the colour give you energy or relax you? Here are few examples of how colour and colour combinations work:

Dress In Red When You Wish
- To express lot of energy and force
- To be seen
- To strengthen your physical side
- To strengthen yourself sexually

Dress In Orange When You Wish
- To motivate yourself
- To react impulsively and let your emotions dictate decisions
- To get in contact with more people
- To have fun and make others and yourself happy

Dress In Yellow When You Wish
- To tell who you are and what you are capable of doing
- To stimulate yourself mentally
- To prevent depression
- To show that you can do more than just the multiplication table

Dress In Green When You Wish
- To ease heartache, and to be kind and good
- To give peace and balance to yourself and others
- To be for other people what you wish other people would be for you

Dress In Blue When You Wish
- To show that you are a wise, good, and spirited person
- To decrease hyperactivity
- To strengthen your analytical and logical side
- To show that you have control over yourself and your surroundings

Dress In Indigo When You Wish
- To stimulate your intuitive side
- To trust your feelings
- To calm your inner confusion
- To show that you have a mystical and mysterious side

Dress In Violet When You Wish
- To be more secure about what you believe in
- To be an ambassador for the violet energy
- To feel inspired and surrounded by helpers

Colour Combinations

In the combinations below, the first colour is the predominant colour and the next colour is the secondary colour.

RED/RED:
An outgoing, vital, and courageous colour combination. It strengthens the desire for new things, such as new challenges at work, friends, travel and new surroundings. This is the energy that will give power to all new creations.

RED/ORANGE:
Strengthens and energizes the physical body. Within this colour combination there is also a wish to help and serve the sick.

RED/YELLOW:
The vigorous, energetic red and helpful, intelligent yellow combine to strengthen your desire to do your best for the benefit of all beings everywhere.

RED/GREEN:
Enhances masculine energy. It helps in harmonizing and energizing all the chakra centres. This is a "give and take" combination (red takes and green gives) A good energy to enhance a person's generous and kind nature.

RED/BLUE:
Brings earth and sky together. The energy strengthens and enhances the ability to use "healing powers," yoga and meditation. It is also the colour energy for "peace on earth."

RED/INDIGO:
Puts together the down-to-earth but ambitious red energy with the indigo's survival instinct of the "sixth sense." The combination protects those who have the desire to explore or those who crave adventure.

RED/VIOLET:
Combines earth elements with spiritual power. The colour is good against any type of evil or bad vibration. The strong vibrations of these two colours cleanse and protect. Clairvoyant people often feel a need for this combination.

The Effect Of Colour

ORANGE/ORANGE:
A good colour combination for before and after an operation. This colour combination is good for everything that has to do with health, food, and sports. This energy has a powerful vital and stimulating effect.

ORANGE/RED:
Orange is a life-loving and optimistic energy. And when it is combined with the brave and lively red energy, it strengthens all activities having to do with competition and sports. But you do not participate just to participate, you want to win.

ORANGE/YELLOW:
This combination creates a "social" energy. You will find it easy to socialize with all types of people. These colour energies like human interaction. Moreover, people are attracted to this energy combination.

ORANGE/GREEN:
Orange energy brings increased interest in social gatherings and all forms of human relationships. Combined with the harmonious and balanced green energy, it creates a good starting point for forming friendships. It also gives energy to those who are in people oriented work.

ORANGE/BLUE:
Indicates self-control, but also a thoughtful caring for others. The orange energy imparts an unselfish and caring happiness in taking care of society's less fortunate.

ORANGE/INDIGO:
Indigo energy encourages intuition and the understanding of things that do not have a concrete answer. This exciting combination enhances and creates new friendships and relationships in which new thoughts and ideas are discussed.

ORANGE/VIOLET:
The happy and outgoing orange energy gives good taste and an aesthetic sense to all kinds of creative work. The combination is also a dream energy and visionary energy that gives people power to wish for more knowledge and wisdom.

The Effect Of Colour

YELLOW/YELLOW:
Yellow is a strong life stimulant that relieves sadness and dark thoughts. Yellow energy is an intelligent, unprejudiced and tolerant colour energy. Yellow strengthens a person's positive and optimistic outlook on life.

YELLOW/RED:
The intellectual person finds harmony in the yellow energy. Combined with the brave and active red energy, it gives strength to those who wish to promote their ideas and theories.

YELLOW/ORANGE:
Sunlight, joy and happiness vibrate in this combination. The yellow energy's intelligent potential and the orange energy's optimism make those thriving in this radiance of positive well-being feel even better.

YELLOW/GREEN:
This combination creates harmony and a feeling of well-being. The yellow energy clears your thoughts and the green energy gives peace and strength to carry out daily tasks.

YELLOW/BLUE:
Are you wondering who you are? This combination strengthens individual potential - who you are and what you should do to be yourself. The colour combination also strengthens recognition of your ego.

YELLOW/INDIGO:
Yellow is a colour that ties people together. In this colour combination there is a wish to unite people with ideas and ideals. Man does not live by bread alone.

YELLOW/VIOLET:
Idealism and mental balance are mixed in this colour combination. Memories, bad experiences, and all fears are washed away by this colour energy.

The Effect Of Colour

GREEN/GREEN:
Green colour energy creates freedom for the "soul." You will quickly get heartaches if you lock up your soul. Green is harmony, balance, peace, and love.

GREEN/RED:
This is a combination that enhances feminine energy. Green gives security and stability, while the red energy gives power and courage. The combination strengthens home and family.

GREEN/ORANGE:
This combination enhances the green energy's simple and uncomplicated efforts with the much involved and eager-to-learn orange energy. A good energy combination for teaching.

GREEN/YELLOW:
The yellow energy's positive attitude towards life releases the green energy's earthbound and practical power. This combination increases and enhances the type of power that clever financial investors need. Money almost grows on trees when in the hands of these individuals.

GREEN/BLUE:
This is a strong, helpful, and kind colour combination. Harmony, balance, tolerance, and patience exist in this mix. Green symbolizes immortality and blue eternal life.

GREEN/INDIGO:
The green colour energy, especially combined with indigo, is good for craftspeople. It gives inspiration to people who work as architects or as artistic craftspeople.

GREEN/VIOLET:
This combination strengthens the "soul" that has found itself. Spiritual energy is a great source of inspiration when the heart is in it.

The Effect Of Colour

BLUE/BLUE:
This is the colour combination that gives people great mental energy. Blue strengthens and gives spiritual nourishment. This colour is good to use when the body's system is over-worked or stressed, resulting in fevers, headaches, insomnia, etc.

BLUE/RED:
Blue is a conservative colour that enhances responsibility and a sense of obligation. Blue combined with the energetic and vital red energy is a good combination for those who are involved in socially responsible activities, and where judgment is connected to action.

BLUE/ORANGE:
Here the blue energy's healing power is combined with the number one health colour. Orange gives happiness and enough energy to enjoy life. This combination imparts knowledge about the meaning of a "healthy soul in a healthy body."

BLUE/YELLOW:
This colour combination gives peace and wisdom. When truth and wisdom are combined, the energy is clear and clean. You will feel mentally cleansed when this energy flows through you.

BLUE/GREEN:
This is the energy of the searcher and the dreamer. The colour combination increases love for all living creatures, the environment, and nature. This is an energy that strengthens the understanding that people have to adapt to nature and its laws.

BLUE/INDIGO:
This combination increases sensitivity to oneself and others. Furthermore, the energy controls passion and enthusiasm. It strengthens you if you wish to go back in time and collect something from your memory.

BLUE/VIOLET:
Blue is a spiritual colour energy. This energy enhances faith and the confidence you need to really have an "open mind." True idealism is strengthened in this combination of blue and the highest spiritual colour, violet.

The Effect Of Colour

INDIGO/INDIGO:
This is the colour of the "third eye." This energy can help you if you want to receive information and intuitive knowledge from your soul. It helps you to feel and understand that there is "nothing new under the sun."

INDIGO/RED:
The indigo energy's intuitive ability to sense and understand combined with the energetic and brave red energy creates a powerful ability to strategize. This combination is great for anything that has to be explored or started. This is the colour combination of "founders" and "initiators."

INDIGO/ORANGE:
This colour combination is an ideal one. The clairvoyant and visionary energy of indigo combined with the happy, humorous, and tolerant orange energy makes for the true bringers of happiness and the artists of life.

INDIGO/YELLOW:
Indigo energy combined with yellow energy creates consideration and caring for others. This energy enhances the interest in new philosophical and universal ideas.

INDIGO/GREEN:
Indigo energy with its need to seek new thoughts and ideas balanced with the harmonious and practical green energy gives nourishment to those who seek stability and tradition. But, at the same time, it helps them to understand that life has to go on, change, and evolve.

INDIGO/BLUE:
This is the colour combination for those who like everything that is aesthetic, beautiful, tasteful, and in perfect harmony. The indigo energy's intuitive sense combined with the blue energy's pure sense of truth helps to unveil the truth behind everything.

INDIGO/VIOLET:
This combination creates an unconventional energy. It is a combination for the individualistic and radical person. Indigo combined with violet enhances the urge to create something no one has either seen or heard about before.

The Effect Of Colour

VIOLET/VIOLET:
Violet colour energy is "healing" for the soul. This energy wishes to serve the earth with peace and love. It gives inspiration to all art forms. Violet also enhances the wish to inform people about seeing "the light."

VIOLET/RED:
This colour combination helps you so that you can see life's possibilities and challenges without fear and insecurity. The combination does not worry about the result of the action. You live here and now, and do not worry about tomorrow.

VIOLET/ORANGE:
This colour combination gives energy and inspiration to artists, the artists of life, and often to geniuses. It makes the energy that creates art in activities such as cooking, pastry making, and flower arranging.

VIOLET/YELLOW:
This is an ideal combination. Violet and yellow combined give energy to the spiritual intellect, in which thoughts and ideas are converted to words and action. It gives energy to maintain high morals, life values and standards.

VIOLET/GREEN:
The violet's spiritual and creative energy is combined with the good, warm and loving green energy. This combination strengthens practical, creative people. It also makes room for great human compassion.

VIOLET/BLUE:
The progressive blue energy wishes for freedom without restrictions and other formal standard laws. Therefore, this colour combination creates the energy of spiritual freedom. Great freedom fighters and humanists gain strength from this colour combination.

VIOLET/INDIGO:
This combination gives energy to great mental and spiritual strength. This energy mix gives the ability to observe and see things that others do not see.

When I write red/orange, for example, it means that the main colour is red, and that orange is a secondary colour. You can easily compose your own colour combinations. For instance, you can take red as the main colour and combine it with a second colour such as yellow, then add a third colour such as violet. In this manner you can make your own colour combinations. You could, for example, set a table with a tablecloth of your main colour, and then add your second combination colour through candles and napkins. There are a lot of different ways to use colour combinations in order to affect yourself and your guests.

Food

In the East, the philosophy of Yin and Yang is connected to everything, including food. The history of food in Eastern and Western countries is very different. Food in the West has moved more and more a negative direction, becoming unhealthy for the body. Many people eat sweets such as cakes, chocolate, and ice cream on a daily basis. The same goes for frozen fast foods, processed foods, and TV dinners. Meat products such as hamburgers, wieners, and all sorts of deli foods have also become daily foods for a great number of people. All this shows that there is not enough knowledge about what food is and what it means to the body.

It is easy to understand why we eat so differently when you look at the Western world's technological and economic development. Part of western economy is based on people's artificial need for fast or processed foods. On the other hand, the East and underdeveloped countries have retained their traditional eating habits. The Western medicine focuses more on taking care of people after they have fallen ill, while the East has focused on preventing illness. Illness prevention includes eating the right foods, which is based on the East's philosophy of food and different kinds of treatments.

Right now there is a lot of interest in and information on alternative food. Even gourmet restaurants have "healthy food" items on their menus now. The followers of Ayurvedic philosophy are specialists on good alternative food. Most people want better and healthier food, but "health food" is often very expensive. Maybe it should be, since products grown in the good old-fashioned way need more time to grow in the ground, and are more vulnerable to insect damage. The result is a

Yang   Yin   Out of balance, illness may start.

In balance, the body is self healing.   Yang   Yin

smaller crop, but what you get is organically grown food without chemicals. It will take a long time to clean up our farmland and are we willing to pay the price? There are a lot of things we can do, and it is starting to become more urgent. Yet, before we start spending too much time and energy on changing the environment, we should start changing our inner environment. The outer change will then happen automatically. As most philosophies state: start with changing yourself bit by bit, before you start changing the whole world.

Food Hints

If you are interested in why you lack vitality, and never feel quite well , or if you know deep down inside that there is something wrong, you should check out some good books on how food affects people. Please refer to the list at the end of this book. Below are a few ideas that may help you.

1. *Start your morning with a glass of lemon juice with a pinch of cayenne pepper and ginger in it, or have a glass of beet and carrot juice.*
2. *About an hour later you may want to eat some light fruit.*
3. *Eat you first meal between 11 am to 1 pm. It should be a high carbohydrate meal with vegetables.*
4. *Supper should be a protein meal with vegetables.*
5. *Drink a lot of water between your meals, but do not drink water with your meals.*

This is all you have to do. I will explain why. Our entire metabolism is not built to digest the complex variety of food we eat at one meal. It is very important to combine the right foods. The food has to be broken down to single biochemical forms before it can be transported to the cells via the blood vessels. This job is performed by enzymes, which are the active elements in the digestive juices. They are responsible for the correct breakdown of the food we eat. For instance, the enzymes that break down fat cannot break down proteins as well. The enzyme that breaks down proteins cannot break down carbohydrates and starch. It becomes easier to understand how to combine foods when you know this. When you combine the wrong foods together it can block the whole digestive system. Poorly digested food can create metabolic toxins. These toxins can create a lot of illness.

Carbohydrates And Starch

Carbohydrates are one of the main sources of energy for the body. Carbohydrates are found in fruit, nuts, seeds and grains. The body converts all sugar and starch to glucose for immediate use, or to glycogen to be stored as energy. Ptyalin and amylopsin are the main enzymes that break down carbohydrates. Carbohydrates and starches are digested by an alkaline digestive juice.

Protein

Protein is the building block of our bodies. It builds and repairs skin and is extremely important to health and vitality. Protein consists of smaller elements called amino acids, which are more complicated than fats and carbohydrates. Enzymes such as pepsin and trypsin are the main forces in the breakdown of protein. Protein needs acid to be digested.

Fat/Oil

Fat is the most concentrated form of energy found in food. Fat consists of carbon, hydrogen, and oxygen. These elements exist in carbohydrates as well, but in different concentrations. Fat also contains the vitamins A, D, E, and K. Fat helps change carotene into vitamin A, and it aids in the process of bringing calcium to the body and skin. Lipase, a fat separating enzyme, breaks fat and oil down to glycerol and fatty acids. Fatty acids are important to normal growth, nerves, arteries, and fresh blood. In the liver the glycerol is transformed into glucose and glycogen, which again is used as energy fuel.

Isn't it fantastic that all this work is going on around the clock without you having to push one single button! Well, you might have to one day if you don't look after your "factory." Then you might have to push a button to get help from a nurse.

What Should I Eat?

Be aware that all the colour energies are represented in the food you eat. Your food should contain a little bit of everything. Everyday you should eat something a little sour, a little salty, a little sweet, and a little bitter. Watch that you combine foods that are right for you. But at the same time, you have to make sure that the food is right for everybody else in the family as well. It will probably be more complicated than buying a readymade chicken dinner to stick in the oven. Hippocrates, the founder of medicine, said "Let food be your medicine and let medicine be your food."

All cultures have used herbs as part of their diets. Herbs are used to help people stay vital, and to cure diseases. We have to start to think differently about what we eat. We do not eat just to satisfy the eye and palate. We need to eat in order to survive. One of the books I would like to recommend is *Eating Alive*, by Dr. John Madsen.

Dr. Randolph Stone, founder of the theory of Polarity, has many good health ideas and exercises to improve health. This recipe for Polarity Tea is one of his ideas. It works on all five excretory systems in the body. It also helps digestion, and in the removal of toxins from the body.

Polarity Tea:

2 tablespoons fennel
1 pinch peppermint leaves
2 tablespoons fenugreek seeds
2 tablespoons linden seeds
2 tablespoons aniseed
3-4 pieces liquorice root
4-5 slices ginger root

Cook the ginger root in a litre of water for three to four minutes. Put all the dry ingredients in a one litre thermos and pour the ginger water into the thermos. Let the tea stand for ten minutes. Drink the tea throughout the day, thinning with boiling water if necessary.

Hints For Healthy Skin

Some people eliminate more toxins through their skin than other people. They can even smell their own bad body odour. This body odour can be removed by first washing the skin with soap. Then prepare a mixture of two thirds baking powder and one third fine-grained sea salt. Put the mixture on a washcloth and scrub your skin while it is wet. It works like fine sand-paper and removes acids stored in your skin. Rinse your skin and while it is still moist, rub it with cold pressed almond oil. Let your skin dry.

We have talked a little bit about the eyes, and how they receive light energy from colours. But the skin is just as important. Not only does the skin receive light and transform it into life essential vitamins, but the skin also breathes and cleanses the body of toxins and excessive gasses. People have to wrap themselves in layers of clothing in a northern climate. This does not let in a lot of light. Often it is only the face and hands that are open to the light and air. Perhaps, you might become more interested in keeping your skin clean if you think of it as one big surface that is constantly exhaling and inhaling. The skin's pores should not be plugged with lotion twenty-four hours of the day. To maintain good health you should scrub your body every day. In fact a good idea is to start everyday with a body scrub. Use a scrub to brush your hands, neck, chest and breasts. Do not forget to scrub your inner and outer thighs. This is where the kidney, gallbladder and liver meridians are located. They really need to be stimulated.

Essential Oils

I can think of nothing more wondrous that taking a *Colour Bath* in which essential oils have been added. This luxury for both body and soul is well worth the extra money the oils cost. Essential oils do not just smell heavenly; but they are beneficial in many ways.

When I started developing the *Colour Baths* I considered adding oils. But the concern for maintaining the therapeutic properties of the colours outweighed any consideration of a nice smell. I have the utmost respect for aromatherapists because of my work with colours. Their knowledge about oils and their uses is most impressive. We actually recommend the use of oils in baths. Nothing is more soothing for body and soul than using *Colour Bath* and essential oils in a bath. But oils like colours have a plus and minus side. One type of essential oil might be good for one person, but not for another, and totally wrong for a third person. And most importantly, you should know the quality of the oil you use. Oils are like wine - there are good years and bad years. Oils can be cheap, expensive, organic, plant-based, or synthetic chemicals. That is why we have made our *Colour Bath* without oils. But we recommend the use of oils in our little booklet *Colour Energy for Body and Soul*. We also sell essential oils separately. Our soaps contain hundred percent pure and extremely high-grade essential oils. Here is an explanation of the beneficial effects of the essential oils we use in our *Colour Energy Bath Soaps*.

YLANG-YLANG
Ylang-Ylang is a sensual and captivating aphrodisiac. It loosens repressed feelings, and is helpful in cases of frigidity and impotence. It helps open the green and violet energy centres. Ylang-Ylang oil stimulates creativity, fantasy, and dreams. It reduces feeling of depression and apathy, and increases self-confidence.

MELISSA
Melissa oil helps to strengthen the nerves, especially when you are suffering from depression, melancholy, and sadness. Furthermore, it is good for headaches and migraines. Melissa oil also can be used for asthma and bronchitis.

The Effect Of Colour

ROSEMARY
Rosemary helps to improve concentration, memory, and creativity. It promotes courage and clarity. Rosemary strengthens the heart and nerves, and helps to relieve muscle and rheumatic pain.

EUCALYPTUS
Eucalyptus is relaxing and balancing. It is excellent when used to cleanse negative vibrations from your surroundings. It is good to put a few drops of eucalyptus oil in hot water and inhale the steam when you have a cold, sore throat or bronchitis. It helps you to relax when taking a bath. It is also good for rheumatism and other joint pains.

GERANIUM
Geranium is an especially calming oil for the nerves. It helps to alleviate depression. Geranium is an antiseptic and a mild pain killer. It is used for stomach problems, enteritis, diarrhea, sores, eczema, and burns.

PATCHOULI
Patchouli is another aphrodisiac that helps to reduce frigidity and impotence. It is a powerful, peaceful, and earthy oil. Patchouli helps you keep your physical body connected to physical reality.

LAVENDER
Lavender brings clarity and peace to the soul. It will help if you are suffering from insomnia, depression, stress, or worry. Lavender oil lowers blood pressure and is beneficial for asthma, bronchitis, colds, coughs, and sore throats. It strengthens the immune system.

We also have not added essential oils to our *Colour Bath*, because pregnant women and people with serious illnesses or allergies should not use certain oils. These people should definitely talk to an aromatherapy specialist first.

Nowadays you can find a lot of books on aromatherapy and essential oils. Just remember that you should use good quality and pure oils. There are many inferior oils on the market today. High quality essential oils are not cheap. You get what you pay for.

ALTERNATIVE THERAPIES

Chromotherapy Or Light Therapy

This type of therapy consists of treating people with coloured light. It is similar to a colour solarium. It is an excellent form of therapy combined with *Colour Bath* bathing.

Acupressure

This is similar to acupuncture, but without needles. The technique is to apply pressure and to massage the points along the body's meridian lines. Chi Tung is acupressure from China. Jin Shin and Shiatsu is the Japanese form of acupressure. It is a superb way of getting rid of emotional blockages.

Acupuncture

Acupuncture has been used in China for over five thousand years. Acupuncture bases its treatment on manipulating people's vital energy or what the Chinese call Chi. Yin and Yang are two complimentary Chi-energies. The Chi-energy is a power that comes from the universe itself. When the Chi-energy is not working properly it can cause an imbalance in the body and ultimately illness.

Yin energy is connected to the feminine principle and is symbolized by the earth, moon, winter, and water. Yang is the masculine principle and is symbolized by the sun, sky, summer, and fire. Yin and Yang are also connected to different organs in our bodies. For example, lungs which are Yin and the large intestine which is Yang are connected through the skin. The heart which is Yin is connected to the small intestine which is Yang through the veins. There are five elements in Chinese medicine: wood, fire, earth, metal and water. These elements are all connected to the body and have their own relationships with one another. Yin and Yang work through the body's twelve main energy meridians and hundreds of smaller channels. The Acupuncture practitioner will first check the client by feeling the pulse of the twelve meridians. Using information from the pulse readings, s/he will make a "situation card." Then s/he will use acupuncture to help the client regain a balance between Yin and Yang.

Kinesiology

A lot of *Colour Energy* customers are kinesiologists. Their system works incredibly well in finding out what colour energy a person needs. Kinesiologists let the body itself tell what it needs. This form of treatment has become more and more recognized and a lot of physiotherapists are now including kinesiology in their treatments.

Polarity Therapy

In Europe several polarity therapists have graduated within the last couple of years. Randolph Stone, the founder of Polarity Theory, has created a form of therapy that I believe is one of the best. There is a lot of good information available on the subject, and there is an association you can contact for further information.

The Caduceus

The Caduceus, often called the wand of Mercury, is an old and mystical symbol of life and death. Originally it came from Egypt, and before that from Atlantis. Today the Caduceus is a symbol of pharmaceutical medicine. But only a very few people in medicine know what it stands for. Long ago teachers of medicine stopped telling about the wisdom its symbolism holds.

The Symbols Of The Caduceus

The round ball at the top of the stick represents the hypothalamus and the pineal gland. The pineal gland is the centre of consciousness and psychic instinct. The double wings symbolize the brain's two parts–primary and secondary. The big double wings represent the main brain with its millions of nerve fibres. This is the thought centre which directs all electrical impulses. The two smaller wings represent the cerebellum, which regulates the autonomic nervous system through the sympathetic system. The stick itself represents the marrow in the spine. The two snakes represent thought or "mind-principle" in its dualistic form, where it passes down the sympathetic system to the tail bone. The snakes meet each other at the chakra points, wherein the nerve centres connect with the sympathetic system in the cerebrospinal. The dense and fine nerve fibres change their polarity at these cross points.

> *I will include a little history:*
>
> *In ancient Greece, students of medicine, learned self-control by being placed in a dugout with numerous poisonous snakes for nine days without food or water. The student's only protection was "the snake within himself"–in his spine. Kundalini power manifests itself in the spine. If the pupil could use this power the snakes would not touch him, as they would consider him one of their own.*

A Little Bit About How We Breathe

When we breathe we inhale energy in the form of positive and negative ions. This breathing in of ions is incredibly important to our lives. Both the left and right nostrils contain a network of microscopic cilia. Researchers say that these cilia are electrically charged. One of their tasks is to give bacteria and similar organisms an electrical charge before they are allowed to enter the body. Cilia in the left nostril are negative and cilia in the right nostril are positive.

The average person breathes approximately fifteen breaths every minute. That makes twenty-one thousand breaths every day, if breathing in a natural rhythm. Usually when you breathe through your nose you only breath through one nostril at a time. You change breathing from your left to your right nostril every other hour. If we inhale a little more than usual we will get a bigger intake of oxygen. And if we inhale even more and use our whole lower body from the stomach up when we breathe, we will be able to benefit from even more oxygen and more ions. This will strengthen the respiration and circulatory systems, and increase the ability of our cells to receive life energy and eliminate waste products. Breathing better and more will give us a more vital life as well as increase our body's consciousness.

7

How Can We Use Our Energies Positively In Our Daily Lives?

I am going to discuss a few of my personal views on the school system, the rising crime rate, and drug abuse, because all of these things affect our daily lives so much. It is quite natural to become interested in what goes on in the world when you work with colour energies and on yourself. In the holistic teachings, it is impossible not to look for the reason behind things.

Kindergarten/School

It is during the school years that the shaping and influencing of future adults takes place. At school the seed is sowed that will determine how well we will fit into society. Of course family also plays an important role. But it is not until the child has to adapt to, and develop in, a greater social context that the child will reflect on what others, including adults and children, think of her or him. In a group of at least twenty children there will probably be at least one each of the seven main colour personalities.

From my time as a kindergarten teacher I remember the typical active, bragging, and tough red child, but also the careful, slightly worried, yet ever so clever and hungry for knowledge yellow child. But at that time I did not know the patterns, or the limitations and the possibilities, of the different colour personalities of the children. It is only now that I realize what I could have done. I could have divided the children into different groups. I could have organized the groups so that each group included one of each colour personality, so that there would be seven different views and behaviours to relate to. I would have understood why the children behaved and acted so differently. I could have taught them teamwork. They could have begun to understand how they depend on each other, and how cooperation creates a functioning team. I could have taught them that one alone is nothing. Everybody is equally important, and when they help each other to stay balanced positively that they really help themselves. This would result in a feeling of self-worth–the feeling that you are somebody, and that the energies and talents you naturally bring to the world are worth something.

It is not better to be bright and intelligent, strong and courageous, musical and creative, than to be kind and good, funny and helpful, sensitive and intuitive. We need all these human qualities.

Loyalty, unsnobbishness, friendship, childish joy, and happiness were the most important things I learned from the children in kindergarten. A base for a good society will be well underway if we teach children to develop into what they were meant to become. Children need to understand that at some point in their lives they will have to and should live in harmony with the seven types of people. If children learn to help each other at school, later in life they will understand that they have to be responsible for each other. As adults in the work force, the same thoughts and actions will result in co-workers being seen as part of the human responsibility. You will take care of each other because, "You help yourself and your society when you help your neighbour." Masonic lodges and other humanistic organizations are founded on this principle. You do not need to be a member of a secret lodge, though, to be helpful, caring, and charitable. It should go without saying. Nobody should have to feel unneeded, worthless, or useless. We all belong together–red, orange, yellow, green, blue, indigo, and violet people. Together we are a rainbow.

Society
Our society is a reflection of who we are. It reflects the energy that we contribute to society and the energy that dominates our daily lives. Since you choose to be either positive or negative, you also choose how you want to affect people, and how you will relate to the community you are a part of. You are most definitely involved with your own life and should, therefore, also see society as a part of that involvement. If you want the society to be involved with you, you must be involved with society. If you wish society to be like a responsible business run by democratically chosen people, and if you wish that taxes and duties should be distributed for everyone's benefit, then you should get involved with your community. We will get the kind of society we deserve.

Drug Abuse

Because we know which types of people have the potential to be drug abusers, let us then intervene at an early stage in their life to prevent any damage. Parents, kindergartens, and schools all have a big responsibility to help children until they are ready to cooperate and understand the dangers of their own energy. We are all responsible for our own lives. I am sure many people would handle their responsibility better if they were only given information on how to manage their energies, and how to understand themselves more.

Schools have conveniently skipped teaching the chapter on how to live, and to understand how we should live. Being born is like a gamble. Where we were born, our nationality, our parents, and our family status are very influential in our development, especially since the school system and society as whole emphasizes a yellow, blue, and green educational system. Our chances of running into problems will be enormously high if we are born as an orange or indigo person, as the odds are then against us. Let the energies, which ever colour energy resource we might have, decide who we are and how to live in society. Let us early on in childhood understand that we function best in a colour community.

Not only do we have the seven main energies, but we also have the seven main types of people with seven different needs for being understood, taught and rewarded. It might be difficult to understand that we all have the seven energies in us. But think about the chakra energy system and how it works. We develop our chakra energy centres when we focus on developing ourselves, whether we use yoga, dance, meditation, prayer, or development courses. The source of all the different ways to develop lie in these centres. We are on our way to becoming whole people when we have learned to use the different centres. It is helpful to understand that we have both a positive and negative side and if we choose not to use the negative side it will be beneficial for us. But it is a bad idea to choose not to understand the negative side. We are not able to help drug addicts until we can truly say that we understand. We must learn to understand that no person is a stranger. It must become part of our knowledge that when an orange or indigo person is on his/her negative side that is when we possibly will get a drug abuser.

The teachings of Jesus are founded on the philosophy that you should help and understand your neighbour. If this teaching is correct and if our society is supposedly built on this principle, then I do not understand why it is not working in reality. Drug and alcohol abuse, and crime is on the increase. Where do we start to correct the problem? Who has to change first, us or the drug abusers?

Think of a group of people climbing a mountain side. They slowly work their way up, making sure that everything is safe before they hoist up the next person. In this way they work their way up, first one, and then the next person. The same goes for our own development. We should take one step at a time, make sure we are balanced, and then help another person up. Going forward alone, without looking back or trying to help someone else is not development, but an ego-trip.

Crime

When a society has a high crime rate, it means that the people who perpetrate the crimes are living and acting on the negative side of themselves. The foundation of a society has to be good in order for the society to develop positively. Lots of good strong energy is wasted on crime. Too many good ideas, courage, and strength go to the negative side. We need this strength. It is often the smart, intelligent, resourceful people who use their energies wrongly. It is society's job to find ways of obtaining a balance for them.

We have to begin to understand how and why people choose to live on the negative side. Our identity and self perception is formed in childhood, but the way others perceive us is extremely important. We are reflected in other people. All people, indeed, all living creatures, wish to be loved and respected.

Criminals can often be divided into two groups. The usual criminal is often a red energy dominated person (today we also have a fair share of orange energy dominated criminals who commit drug related crimes). The "white collar" criminals are mostly blue energy dominated. How they perceive themselves determines their choices in life. Likewise, there are experiences from childhood that can create negativity and blockages. Later on in life, they could have been met with a lack of understanding, or they could have become involved in something due to unforeseen reasons. This is the same pattern you will see in emotional blockages or in illnesses. The people are caught in their own nets.

We have to use our own resources and our knowledge about people to prevent other people from getting into situations where they use their negative energies. What is the use of building strong prison walls, and increasing the police force if we cannot protect people? The resources first must be used in understanding people, then we can start the preventative work. There is a reason for this–we cannot leave to the next generation a world that accepts an increasing crime rate as part of a normal society. This would be ruinous and fatal.

How Can We Use Our Energies Positively In Our Daily Lives?

"All that evil requires to flourish, is for good men and women to do nothing!"

I think that when a judge is deciding a case, it would be a good idea to let a convicted criminal act as assisting judge, since the convict and the person on trial come from the same kind of environment. Only a person serving a similar sentence can help other people understand the reason the crime was committed. S/he would also gain insight about her/his own sentence. Likewise, s/he would help give somebody the right sentence. We are not just punishing a criminal, we also have to help him or her.

Illness And Health

I would put money into the pharmaceutical industry today, if I wanted to invest in an industry with a growing and secure future. I have always been and still am very impressed by research on, for example, micro-organisms, or the incredible inventions that help us to understand and help the human body. But the system is all wrong. All the work is concentrated around the sick person. I think that health services should focus on prevention. People should be taught to take responsibility for their own machinery. You must look at yourself as a factory. You have a body and you have everything you need in this body. In your body there is a power station from which you receive your energy. You have a feeding facility and a cleaning system. You are constantly going to school or taking part in educational training. Throughout your life there are "assignments" which you must complete. You let your body work to keep your own machinery running. And that is what it is all about–your industry, your power station, and your body. Let's use the words "your energy" instead of "your health." What is important for you and your body is what kind of energy your choose and how you use it. Of course you will experience bad circulation, accumulations, constipation, and finally blockages in your machinery if you eat and drink the wrong energy. Many people eat fried food, microwaved food, and too much meat every day. Likewise, people's diets include white bread, white sugar, coffee, alcohol, beer and too many dairy products, such as milk and cheese. It is inevitable that something will go wrong: maybe it will not happen when you are twenty, but most certainly at fifty.

Health services should concentrate on making new systems in which the purpose is to map out the newborn human being. Which type of person is the newborn? The eastern Ayurvedic system divides people into three types. This alone would be very helpful. We are all different and food that is good for one person, may not be good for another. We do not need the same energy, no matter how much we like the same food.

How Can We Use Our Energies Positively In Our Daily Lives?

Do you know what type of energy you need? Meat is of greater importance to a red person than to an indigo person. You also have to consider your own particular situation. If you normally don't do a lot of physical activity, but you know that over the next few weeks you will be expending quite a lot of physical energy, then you should consider eating red food, and drawing on red energy. You need to fuel your body with the energy you are going to use, and this energy has nothing to do with what you *feel* like eating. Cravings seduce you all the time–it's okay to be seduced on the weekend, but not all week! This seducing–energy does not think of what you need, only of what you like. Most people have become slaves of a seductive, irresponsible, demanding and never satisfied energy, popularly called "I eat what I feel like eating." You do not have to repress this energy totally, as it is good to have a sense of taste, and it is a good friend to have at social events.

But, back to the energy you need. You need different minerals, vitamins, proteins, and carbohydrates in the correct proportions in order for the body to function at a normal speed. At normal speed the body is balanced. If you need to go into a higher gear you have to know you have enough fuel. Many people gear up and go at top speed for a period of time without having filled the reserve or watched that they have enough and the right supply of energy. If you do this the machinery will take energy from all the storage places and reserves, and actually steal energy from other organs until there is no energy left. A breakdown, either physically or psychologically, will often be the result. The most common reaction is tiredness, weakness, the feeling of being drained of energy, and a loss of desire to do anything.

Vitality means the trinity of body, soul, and mind are in balance. It is a wonderful intoxicating feeling to have full vitality. Everything works and the whole body experiences well-being. This should be the normal state of being. Of course something can happen, but that is usually a sign that something is wrong. If you look at your mishaps, symbolically there is always something to learn, especially when you look at it retrospectively. If you are seriously ill and feel that your illness is unfair or too restrictive, you should remember that you can always learn from the situation you are in and use it for further growth and development. All people will meet some trying situations, either mentally or physically, here on earth. There is a lesson to be learned if the body is restricted due to trials and pain. This lesson teaches you that you can separate your body from your thoughts and your soul, and that free thought and a free soul can conquer pain and physical sufferings. The priority you give your different energies is crucial. If your body is the only part that is handling the pain and the illness, then it will be too much of a burden. In this case your "spirit" is very important. Your spirit is the highest form of energy on our earth. There are numerous stories about how "spirit" has conquered a restricted body.

How Can We Use Our Energies Positively In Our Daily Lives?

Take for example Stephen Hawkins, a genius who works from a wheelchair. He became ill in his twenties. At twenty-eight he was appointed math professor at Cambridge University in England. At this point he could neither walk, write, or eat by himself. His head was always hanging down on his chest and if he tried to lift it, it would fall down again. His voice was blurred and muffled, and only those who knew him well could understand what he was saying. From his wheelchair he produced his theory about the universe, "the theory of everything." Hawkins who is now in his fifties has reconsidered a part of this theory. Now he thinks that the fundamental objects in the universe consist of vibrating super threads. He thinks he still needs twenty to twenty-five more years to work on his theory so he can understand it better. On a television program he said, "You can find out how the universe works and why it is like it is. But why it is there, that is more difficult to understand. If we knew that, we would know everything. Then we would know God's thoughts and purpose."

Growth and development happen on different levels, and it is no use feeling unfairly treated by destiny. You have chosen it yourself. Your are responsible for your life, from before you were born until what you become. Reincarnation explains it this way:

You yourself have chosen the life you live.
You yourself have chosen the environment.
You yourself have chosen the challenges you will meet.
You yourself have chosen the assignments you will get.

If you understand this, life will become much more exciting. You will understand that there is a purpose to all that happens. You will know that you came to this earth prepared. Nothing will happen to you that you cannot solve. It gives a certain sense of security knowing that you can solve all your assignments if you want to. There is nothing scary and frightening in front of you. It is only your own thoughts that create barriers.

When you start to clean up your machinery, you will see how shiny clean a liver and a bowel wall can become. When you realize that the food is being processed by enzymes and not just gulped down with drinks every time you take a bite, you will then understand that perhaps indigestion pills and powders are a waste of money. You might even start to have respect for your "fantastic machinery." Your body is the world's only self-healing, self-adjusting, and self-maintaining factory. Yes, that is something to be proud of! These days I meet many people who are almost proud of being sick. They can entertain a whole group of people with stories of their illnesses. When they speak about medicines, they are definitely the best ambassadors the pharmaceutical industry can ask for. These are people that are not interested in themselves, or in becoming well. Most of them can usually get rid of their illnesses if they really want to. It will cost them not just in monetary terms but also in time and interest.

It is often the task of a researcher or a detective to find out what the body reacts to. When that mystery is solved you can go back to the events or the sequences that initialized the emotional blockages, and which, in the end, materialized as a physical illness. You can do this work alone. But you might need help to loosen up the blockages in your body. A good reflexologist, acupuncturist, or polarity therapist can do wonders. You will see faster results if you are active in the treatment and admit to yourself and your body that you could not handle the assignment that started the back-up. It is like in all other types of drains. If one thing gets stuck it will obstruct other things, and everything will get stuck at the same place until it is finally plugged. Our body's energy systems work the same way. But in this case, we are talking about feelings and thoughts–unresolved hidden thoughts and feelings we do not wish to look at. They are the denied feelings and thoughts we wish to forget, thoughts we do not dare live and feelings we do not dare acknowledge. Where do you think all these thoughts and emotions are stored? Does the body store unresolved thoughts and feelings? Yes, the body has space for storing things it does not need including knowledge and experience, and any surplus fuel or energy. I think the core of illnesses is hidden here. The body temporarily stores pent-up feelings and repressed thoughts. The body tries to get rid of some of them through dreams, but if that does not work, the unreleased feelings and thoughts become a pattern repeated over and over again in dreams and nightmares. Emotional blockages try to resolve themselves through dreams before they actually become permanently entrenched in your body. The next step is for the unresolved emotions and thoughts to warn you on the physical level, as joint pains, sore muscles, allergies, or eczema. Now your body is telling you something is wrong. Illnesses that stem from psychosomatic causes are now being recognized by doctors. But all illnesses, of course, do not stem from psychosomatic causes or emotional blockages. Illnesses can be caused by extreme wear and tear of the body, inheritable diseases, and viruses. We can prevent some of these illnesses by making sure the body's immune system is fully prepared. When we realize that we have an elite troop in our bodies, whose main assignment is to unsparingly kill invaders, we should give the elite soldiers first class treatment. Do we make sure that our body's housing for the elite troop is in good condition, or that the food they need is full of energy? No, I do not think so. Today, thanks to successful operations like "Pills and Syringes Ltd., people rely too much on what are considered the leading wonder drugs, antibiotics and penicillin. These medicines were invented to save lives, and not to kill the body's elite soldiers. But nowadays, people take antibiotics on a regular basis for just fevers and sore throats. We have built a society in which the use of drugs creates a vicious circle. This is a typical scenario:

> *If a child is sick for too long, it will create problems for the parents who have to work. They will give the child medicine so that the child gets well quickly. But because the immune system never recovers fully, the child gets quickly sick again. The parents then have to buy more medicine, so that the child will get well quickly, so that the parents do not miss work, and so on.*

The body prefers to heal itself, but it usually takes a little longer than if antibiotics are used. The body has an elite troop, and even if it seems as if one battle is lost there are hidden energy reserves to draw from. The body will heal itself if it is given time, and the right treatment and surroundings. But we are too impatient. We do not have time to wait. We therefore choose the easiest way, which in the end might become the most difficult. I know it sounds very depressing, but maybe researchers will eventually find new means to strengthen the elite troops. I am a big admirer of research and the development of new medical products, but I do not approve of everybody using these products. You have a choice when you are dealing with your own life.

We have to try to change the way we look at illnesses. Illnesses do not come from the outside nor are they unexpected or uninvited. They come from within. They usually have been there for a long time, and have announced their arrival several times both "in writing" and "verbally." When will we take our illness seriously, and understand that illness tells us that we are living incorrectly, and that we are on the negative side of ourselves? I hear many people say: "I can't help that I am sick. The doctor says I am sick. It might be incurable. I am sick..."

Ayurveda
Ayurveda is a practical philosophy and lifestyle that has existed for more than five thousand years in India. Ayurveda, in Sanskrit, means "the science of life." Ayurveda teaches that a person is a microcosmo, a universe in itself. According to Ayurvedic teachings a person has four biological and spiritual instincts: religion, economy, reproduction and freedom. These four instincts can be developed correctly if you remain balanced and in good health. Ayurveda helps a healthy person stay healthy, and a sick person become healthy again. I believe it is worthwhile to read books on the Ayurvedic system. You will learn to understand and take care of your own health. Good health is an individual responsibility. You should not leave your health up to the government, health services, or society in general.

Healing

Even though some words have negative connotations, it is often better to use the original word. The word "healing" is easily understood by anyone who has taken even the slightest interest in alternative therapies. Nowadays the concept of "healing" is used in public healthcare, but it is called "pain relief." Fingers and hands are charged with energy, and if doctors and nurses were aware of the power and force of healing hands, they could do double the wonders. A lot of people use these abilities without knowing it. People have probably said to them, "You have such good warm hands. It is so nice when you touch me. It is as if I feel better just having you here." The people who fit this description have the ability to let energy flow out to heal others. Energy, in fact, flows the most easily out through our fingers.

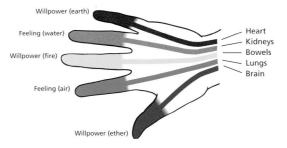

A truly positive attitude is incredibly important to maintain a physically strong defense against illnesses. By having a positive and open attitude you receive different forms of energy, from food and drink to sound and light energy coming from the universe. You might ask though, "What about environmental things we have no control over? What about chemical and radioactive pollution, noise pollution, stress, moral poisoning, and the influence of violence on our lives?" I could go into a lengthy explanation, as a lot research is being done to find solutions, but I would rather answer that the fear of what could happen has probably hurt people more than the actual danger. People are too paranoid or neurotic in today's society. Good mental health and a positive attitude will support the immune system. Remember the old saying, "A healthy soul in a healthy body."

Beauty And Health

Here are a few tips on how to take good care of your skin. Remember that beauty comes from within. But we can teach ourselves a few tricks. Then when we look at ourselves in the mirror, or at other people, we will know a little bit more about why we and others look so tired or feel terrible.

When you have pale skin, dark circles under your eyes, and when you look tired, you need the red energy. Red energy will make your blood flow out to your skin.

How Can We Use Our Energies Positively In Our Daily Lives?

Your skin will glow with warmth. The red energy, which you find in beets and liver for example, will strengthen your blood and the blue circles under your eyes will disappear.

You need the orange energy if your suppleness and enthusiasm for life is gone, and if you feel under the weather. The orange energy will give you vitality. It will help you to enjoy life "right now," and it will make you feel like laughing and dancing.

You need the yellow energy if your eyes are tired, and if they look more like expressionless fish eyes than shiny human eyes. The yellow energy will return the sparkle to your eyes, for your eyes are the mirror of your soul. If you have a lot of positive yellow energy, people will be able to tell right away.

You might need the green energy if your smile is stiff, your lips tight, and your lipstick dry and cracked. When the green energy flows through your heart, which beats to make others happy, you will smile at the world. With the green energy your smile will become soft, happy, and a warm energy will flow from you.

If your head feels like cotton, everything buzzes, and your thought and words are confused, you need the blue energy. The blue energy will give you concentration, clarity, and control over your thoughts and actions.

If you feel lonely, or that nobody really understands you, then you need the indigo energy. The indigo energy will give you a feeling of being part of the universe. Everything has a soul, so even animals and flowers can become your friends. This feeling of being connectedwill reflect in your personality.

You might need violet if the day seems long and life dreary and difficult to live. You lack the spark for life. The violet energy will give you inspiration and a feeling of being very special as indeed you are!

The Seven Deadly Sins
Throughout time a few harmful qualities have always been a part of human nature. It is just as important for our health to cultivate positive thoughts and attitudes as it is to avoid bacteria or accidents.

Sloth • Envy • Lust • Gluttony • Pride • Anger • Covetousness

These are difficult qualities. But if you know that these qualities are only negative energy, you can do something about them. You can actually become healthy. You can decide to go to the positive side of these qualities.

8

OUR FUTURE WITH COLOURS

Who knows the future? People with strong indigo energy can know the future. They are able to access all information. Writers, film producers, and others connected to science fiction ideas use their indigo energy. Some people call it using the "big imagination." Think of such writers as Jules Verne, H.J. Wells, and George Orwell. Most of their futuristic visions have become reality. Or think of cartoons like the Phantom and Flash Gordon. Much of what was once fantasy has become fact. Nowadays we have shows such as Star Wars, Star Trek, and Deep Space Nine. These shows have given us some insight into what life could be like in the future. Whatever the human mind can imagine, humans can make reality. This is true for both a positive or a negative direction. Energy is simply energy, neither positive or negative in itself. But we can choose whether to use it in a positive or negative fashion. Inspiration, ideas, and power are energy, but what they produce will depend on how they are used.

Positive Energy Creates:	Negative Energy Creates:
Joan of Arc	Jack the Ripper
Martin Luther King	Adolf Hitler
Nelson Mandela	Josef Goebbels
Rigoberta Manchu	Idi Amin

In the aftermath of a war much research is conducted on war equipment, from weapons to clothing. These things are first produced for a negative purpose, but they also can be useful. Then objects that were once made for war are later used for peace. The race to be the first to conquer space virtually guarantees that we will inhabit other places in this universe. It is up to us to create the kind of future we will have. Whether our world is at war or peace depends on whether we who are living in peace are willing to sacrifice more than just a few dollars to maintain and spread peace.

Our future is in our thoughts. Our thought patterns will shape our society. Consciousness is a word nobody can explain. We can discuss in length what consciousness means to different people, but the Biblical expression, "man know yourself"would be the closest to the truth. Copernicus and Einstein changed our view of the universe. Darwin and De Jardin changed our perception of our role in the universe. Freud and Maslow changed how we look at ourselves. What is going to happen in the future? Will researchers, philosophers and people change their view on consciousness? Will everybody understand that we are a perfect part of an incredibly perfect system? And will everybody understand that we have to live in peace with one another to become a part of the rainbow connecting sky and earth?

Medicine Of The Future

The medicine of the future could become light. We could enter a bright time, where a surgeon's scalpel is replaced by a laser. Colours would be prescribed instead of pills. Acupuncture needles would be needles of coloured light. Illnesses would be cured because we would understand that the body, soul, and mind are one, and we would create treatments accordingly. The new medicine would treat people, not illnesses. And the new medicine would not just treat the symptoms of the illness, but the actual cause. It could be the medicine of a holistic era, in which doctors would work with energies, both visible and invisible, with a new understanding that the world we cannot see and understand, is just as important as what we see and understand!

9

A Few Words About Myself

I am educated as a kindergarten teacher and this book grew out of my experiences with children. But it was when I reflected back on my own childhood, I realized that I shared many similar qualities with my classmates. It made me both happy and sad that we were all so alike. I was happy, because I understood that there were more people like me. And sad, because I found out that the school and many of the parents, including my own, did not want to understand why we are like we are. But most of all I was sad, because of all the wasted years lying ahead of all these children.

I quit teaching kindergarten because I felt I did not have anything to offer. I did not have any good ideas on how to change the system. That is why I felt it was maybe better to quit. Years went by: I married, had three children, and divorced. For years I worked in various places, but all the time I was moving ahead and learning. I was lucky enough to travel all over the world, meeting many important people connected with alternative ideas. I read, studied, and collected all the information I stumbled upon, about people and their relationship with the inner and outer world. Still I feel that this is just the beginning of our understanding of human beings, light, and colours.

For many years I worked importing clothes from Mexico and Guatemala. After this I began producing clothes made in Norway. The colours of the clothing were of great importance to me. I found I received great pleasure in coordinating colours. The turning point happened on the day I finished making a collection of pink woolen coats. Pink! I had not worn pink since I was a baby. And I had never understood people who swore by the colour pink. I became bewitched and obsessed. "Think pink" was my motto. That year I received proof that there is something called the "collective consciousness." The pink event made me go in the right direction. Little by little, colours and I met. I found the right books, the right people, and the right thoughts started flowing freely. Now I understand all the roads and stopping points in my life, and I am back where I started, in the kindergarten. The circle was completed.

A Few Words About Myself

I find the children in the colours. I recognize myself and others in the colours. I see people as red, orange, yellow, green, blue, indigo, and violet energies. I see their complexity, their distinctive characteristics, their possibilities, and their limitations. And I love them all. A part of each and everyone of them is me, and I am a part of all the others.

My Own Test

DATE OF TEST:	*15.10.1993*
NAME:	*Inger Naess*
DATE OF BIRTH:	*31.08.1936*
ADDRESS:	*Oslo, Norway*
OCCUPATION:	*Designer and Colour Therapist*
FAVOURITE COLOUR:	*All the colours of the rainbow according to need*
LEAST LIKED COLOUR:	*Unclear and cloudy mixed colours*

ORDER	MAIN COLOUR	POINTS
1.	*Violet*	*17*
2.	*Yellow*	*14*
3.	*Red*	*13*
4.	*Blue*	*12*
5.	*Green*	*6*
6.	*Indigo*	*6*
7.	*Orange*	*4*

Here Is The Results Of My Own Test And Its Analysis:

The first thing to notice is the four willpower energies at the top of the list. It points to a person who uses willpower more that feelings. Violet has a message to give or a job to do when it is at the top of the list. To do this job properly I am dependent on whether the energy is positive or negative. As a consultant, I can never tell someone else whether their energy is positive or negative. I can only answer for myself. I think that I am doing reasonably well in keeping the violet energy balanced–this energy is my driving force and I wish to feel its inspiration more than anything else. The positive side is that there is always a flow of good ideas, while the negative side is that I end up doing everything and not really concentrating on what is the most important. I have to work on being in balance everyday. I need to keep myself on track.

A Few Words About Myself

The yellow colour accentuates my curiosity and my urge to always learn more, but I am not a typical yellow. I have an uneasy solar plexus that bothers me at times. I get "butterflies" in my stomach very easily, and I quickly become worried when I experience things I cannot do or have no control over. The controlling willpower energy often chokes my feelings in the yellow centre. As a child I spent a lot of energy practicing to control my feelings such as sadness, fear and pain. I played mostly with boys, and at the time I wished I was a boy. Later I learned to control lots of things, and no one can tell me now that it is less difficult to let go of control than to gain control. Information about the yellow centre should be passed on as early in life as possible. Understanding the yellow centre is the key to preventing many psychosomatic illnesses.

I always feel at home with red people–even if they are on their negative side. I use the red energy in a positive manner since the distance from idea to action is seldom very far for me. I like to use the red energy, and to feel the strong, vital strength that pours out from this action-energy. Of course many see red people as steadfast, decisive, and often stubborn, and unshakable. But these people are not on the negative side. They are in balance. Without these characteristics red people would be wishy-washy; they would be very easy to persuade and they would surrender to pressure way too fast. The strong faithful red would not longer be so strong and faithful. Well, there is something to the saying that you have to take the bad with the good.

The blue energy gives me a lot and I always try to keep it in balance. I am not a typical blue either, and there have been many years where I have consistently tried to avoid the blue energy. Furthermore, there are times when I find it difficult to adjust to the blue energy, especially unbalanced blue people. And believe it or not, there are many of them in our society. The difference between unbalanced red and blue people is that red people create more physical and visible problems in society, while blue people, just like moles, can destroy society with their manipulations. Their lust for power and their cool calculating abilities take over and they end up using their qualities in the wrong way. There are actually not enough positive blue people. We need more of them. I have taken a lot of blue baths, because there are so many good positive blue qualities to draw from, and I would like to enhance these.

Green and indigo are definitely not my strong sides. I am not a typical green, and I lack a lot of the green's great qualities. I would love to have these qualities, but a long time ago I accepted that that's just not the way I am. I am married to a green man, and I thrive in the company of green people. I seek green surroundings, and take green baths. Everyday, I work on keeping my heart chakra open, and that is not easy. I realize that a closed green centre is the most harmful thing that can happen to a person, both physically and psychologically.

Indigo is my conscience and my best friend. Here is the core of my inner understanding. I am absolutely sure that I have my indigo energy balanced. I am actually on the plus side here. I understand the indigo energy, both on the plus and minus side, and I see my "indigo" as a great source from which I can draw energy. I have full confidence in what I receive, as long as I stay balanced and use the energy positively. I was on the negative side of indigo at one time, and I had nightmares and bad dreams. But I learned from that. If you believe in angels, there must be devils also. It is exciting to use your imagination to see both the grotesque and the romantic, but you have to cut loose from fear and anxiety.

Orange is at the very bottom, but that does not worry me too much. I know what I have to do. I do not need the orange creative energy because I have enough violet energy. What I need from the orange energy is happiness and zest, and not to forget the orange energy's unique ability to exist in the here and now. The strong point of the orange is its capacity to be happy about every day. My morning bath is usually orange. I do my best to be in better contact with the joyful orange qualities. I would like to live a life in happiness without having to worry too much about world problems. I try to see myself as a lily under God's sky. Personally I don't think that lilies worry too much.

Introduction To Other Books.

I love books. I see books as my personal friends. Behind their covers are life, experience, and knowledge. Some books are my favourites, and some I do not care so much about. But all of them have touched me. My motto has always been "do not judge the book before you have read it all" and this is what I have done. It is only natural that I have chosen books about light and the colour world, since this is what my book is based on and about. Some books are very specialized, while others talk about life philosophies.

Why You Are Who You Are
Graham Benard

Jonathan Livingston Seagull
Richard Bach

Health and Light
John. N. Ott

The Light-Medicine of the Future
Jacob Liebermann

The Test

What Colour Are You?
Lilla Bek

All the books by Carlos Castaneda

Dreamcards
Strephon Caplan Williams

Ayurveda–the Science of Selfhealing
Dr. V. Lad

Form, Sound, Colour and Healing
Theo Gimbel

Colour Psychology and Colour Therapy
Farber Birren

Gifts of the Gemstone Guardians
Ginny and Michael Katz

Fit for Life
Marilyn and Harvey Diamond

And There was Light
Jacques Lusseyran

The Lost Books of the Bible and the Forgotten Books of Eden

Food Is You Best Medicine
Dr. Henry Bieler

Silva Method
Jose Silva

The Tibetan Book of Living and Dying
Sogyal Rinpoche

How I Read And Mark The Test.

The test consists of both questions and statements. Mark the correct square–"yes"–"sometimes"–"no" with an X. Here are some answers to questions you might have about this test.

Why is the test so long? There are a lot of questions to answer.
Because the more questions I have to work with, the more sure I am of giving you the right answer.

Why do you ask so much about sex?
Sex is an important part in a person's life. Your attitude towards sex says a lot about you. It is therefore very important to be honest with yourself when you answer the questions.

Several questions are misleading. I could answer yes to one part and no to the other part. What do I do?
If you cannot answer yes to the complete question, but only to half of it, you must put your X in the "sometimes" square.

Before you start, remember this: When you answer "yes" the answer must be true seventy-five to one hundred percent of the time. If not, you must answer "sometimes." It is very important to the results that you answer correctly. Your answers reflect how you are today. How you were previously, or what you wish to be, has no significance. The answers should reflect how you are *today*.

The Test

If you take the test seriously and work towards being more balanced, it will be possible to change your energies, or to use more of a particular colour energy than you have in the past.

To receive your own personal *Colour Energy* chart, send the completed COLOUR ENERGY® test with a cheque or money order in the amount of $29.95 (shipping & handling included) to:

> COLOUR ENERGY CORPORATION
> P.O. BOX 1743, STATION A
> VANCOUVER, BC CANADA V6C 2P7

You will receive the results of the test in the form of a colourful chart that lists the seven colour energies you use in their descending order. Our Colour Energy test is used by many professionals all over the world to help people understand themselves better. All answers are held in the strictest confidence and are destroyed after the test results are charted. Allow 3-4 weeks for delivery. For additional copies of the test, please send a SASE with your request to the above address.

TEST

Name: _____

Address: _____

_____

Date of Birth: _____ Occupation: _____

Your favourite colour: _____ Date of Test: _____

The colour you dislike the most: _____

Colour Energy Corporation is a leader in offering a line of wellness products: Colour Bath™ envelopes, Colour Bath bottles, essential oils, scented Colour Energy soaps, *Colour Energy for Body & Soul* booklet. Many more Colour Energy products to come...

Colour Energy products are sold in health, new age, metaphysical, gift and bookstores. For more information call **1-800-225-1226**, E-mail: **colour@colourenergy.com** or visit our web site at **http://www.colourenergy.com**

The Test

	Yes	Sometimes	No
Do you like to study and do you enjoy attending seminars and courses? Are you often occupied with things that interest you on an intellectual level?			
Do you have a lot of friends and do you enjoy interacting with them in a positive way?			
Do you enjoy sharing your happiness with others?			
Do you enjoy good food that you do not necessarily prepare yourself?			
Do you express your feelings in appropriate situations by laughing, crying, or being afraid?			
Do you reason things out quickly, and have a practical grip on your life?			
Do you handle money well?			
Do you have a tendency to ignore your body?			
Are you considered to be optimistic, trustworthy, and full of humour?			
Do you enjoy reading, and are you considered to be an intellectual?			

	Yes	Sometimes	No
Do you enjoy speaking with all types of people because you look for knowledge and wisdom in everything?			
Do you usually find more than one solution to a problem?			
Do you often seem distracted to other people because you are preoccupied with your own thoughts?			
Are your opinions and thoughts considered wise, and do you show your wisdom through your own actions?			
Do you enjoy mental challenges?			
Are you clever at analyzing a situation, and are you capable of solving the problem quickly?			
Do you like being alone, and do you enjoy your own company?			
Are people confident that you can be impartial in a crisis or in negotiations?			
Can you sometimes be a Dr. Jekyll and a Mr. Hyde–warm and open one moment, and skeptical and cold the next?			

The Test

	Yes	Sometimes	No
Do you have a tendency to abuse at least one of the following: prescription drugs, narcotics, alcohol, cigarettes, coffee, chocolate, sweets, sex, sports, hobbies, food, or wine?			
Do you participate in physical exercise such as dancing, or sports such as tennis, squash, swimming, or anything that is fast and energetic?			
Do you enjoy working with your hands in a creative way such as painting, sculpting, ceramics, sewing, or carpentry?			
Do you enjoy physical work more than mental work?			
Do you look younger than your age, and do you seem childlike and innocent?			
Do you think sex is fun?			
Are you impulsive and spontaneous, and do you enjoy making other people laugh and play?			
Do you think it is important to have fun, to play, and to take an active part in being with other people?			
If you encounter a conflict would you rather avoid the situation?			

	Yes	Sometimes	No
Do people think that you are preoccupied with yourself?			
Do you like to learn new things, but you often do not finish the things you start?			
Do you think that you give a good massage, as you feel that your hands can do good for others?			
Do you resent being told what to do because you like to make decisions yourself?			
Do you resent your responsibilities and obligations?			
Do you want to be free to choose according to your mood at the moment?			
Do you think sex is good and that it helps you to relax physically?			
Do you feel at times that you can not cope with your problems? Do you try to avoid your problems by sleeping, moving away, or by becoming sick?			
Are you a good problem solver due to your ability to be creative?			
Do you have a well developed sense of smell? Are you sensitive to the smells of other people? Do you like to smell the food before you start eating?			

The Test

	Yes	Sometimes	No		Yes	Sometimes	No
Are home and family life two of the most important things to you?				Is it easy for you to get things to grow?			
Are you practical with money and do you like secure investments?				Is nature and living a peaceful and harmonious life important to you?			
Would you like a secure job with a stable and steady income?				Are you a good host/hostess and do you like to take good care of your guests?			
Would you enjoy being part of an organization that helps to strengthen or improve the environment of your neighbourhood?				Do you have a tendency to take on too much responsibility and become overloaded with work?			
Are you open, optimistic, and very friendly? Do you cry easily because you are romantic and sentimental? Is it easy for you to let go of your feelings when you are happy, hurt, or angry?				Do you like to work for and with the environment and nature?			
				Are you scared of success, because other people might think that you are preoccupied with yourself?			
Do you feel guilty when you say "no" to someone?				Are you worried that you may not have enough money for your daily needs?			
Do you like to take care of people and are you overprotective?				Do you often feel that people are taking advantage of you, and that they do not appreciate you for everything that you have done for them?			
If a conflict arises do you prefer to resolve the issue by saying "we have to love each other"?				Did you marry or do you want to get married, because a good and solid relationship is important to you? To be alone in depressing.			
Do you easily see the good in people and understand and forgive them?				Do you like hugs and kisses more than the sexual act itself? Is sex only for the physical satisfaction meaningless to you?			

The Test

	Yes	Sometimes	No
Do you like to listen to your inner voice, and do you trust what your body tells you?			
Do you believe that there is spiritual energy in everything around you?			
Do people enjoy your company and come to you for comfort and advice?			
Do you think it is often difficult to be alive?			
You would never lie, steal, or cheat someone as that is an unethical behaviour?			
Is money unimportant to you, as you can survive by other means?			
Do you like to work under other people and give them loving support?			
Nobody needs to tell you what is right or wrong. You know it.			
Do you easily understand masculine and feminine energy, both physically and psychologically?			
Do you comprehend spiritual laws better than physical laws?			

	Yes	Sometimes	No
Do you have a difficult relationship with your own physical body?			
Are you very sensitive and full of emotions, but still strong and independent?			
Do you sometimes feel that you have a healing power that you are not using?			
Do you feel that you do not know what your purpose on this planet is?			
Are you full of imagination and creativity, but you have problems finishing a project?			
Do you need a lot of time for yourself in meditation, or in trying to find and understand yourself?			
Do you sense other people's moods?			
Do you seek the good in everything you do, because without love everything feels meaningless?			
Can your ideas often seem unrealistic? Do you always look for the truth and reality in things?			

The Test

	Yes	Sometimes	No		Yes	Sometimes	No
When you socialize with other people do you prefer activities such as games, dancing, playing and competitions, rather than a discussion on feelings and spiritual matters?				Are you straight forward and often come across as too direct?			
Do you prefer work and hobby projects that give fast and immediate results?				Do you only believe in things that you can see, feel, and have proof of their existence?			
Do you prefer to solve problems with physical action instead of theorizing on the many ways to solve the problem?				Do you take the initiative to start new projects?			
Are you persistent and hard-working? Are you able to get people to work together as a team?				At times do you lose your self-control and become furious and extremely angry?			
				Can you perceive when a situation is potentially dangerous, and are you capable of getting out of the situation?			
Do you have a physical appetite when it comes to sex, food and drinking? Do you enjoy earthly pleasures the most?				When you have decided something and think that your suggestion is the best, do you keep that attitude no matter what resistance you encounter?			
Do you have a temper, but calm down quickly?				For you sex is natural and gives you physical pleasure. You can not understand anybody that does not want to talk or make jokes about it.			
When you have arguments and disagreements with other people, do you resolve them quickly with no hard feelings?							
Are you a loner?				Do you have to feel free to explore and develop yourself sexually, and if this is denied do you get frustrated?			
Do you have a problem with expressing your feelings to others?							
Are you energetic and do you have a lot of self-confidence? Are you independent?				Do you sometimes feel frustrated, and that things are going against you; such as, work, health, money, and relationships? Is everything a struggle?			

The Test

	Yes	Sometimes	No
Do you usually solve your problems in a logical and calm way?			
Are you conservative in the way you dress and in your opinions?			
Is it hard to beat you in a discussion since your arguments are well-documented with statistics and sound logic?			
You do not admit mistakes easily.			
Are you a quick learner and do you understand things well? Do you like to do things your own way?			
Do you like to have control over your feelings, surroundings, friends, and family?			
Do you like to keep yourself slim and in shape? Do you feel being overweight is a lack of self-discipline?			
Are you self-critical and afraid of failures?			
Do you need to know that you will be admired, respected, and loved before you enter into a sexual relationship?			

	Yes	Sometimes	No
Do people readily come to you for advice on their feelings?			
Do you have a tendency to be a workaholic?			
Do you expect a lot of yourself; are you a bit of a perfectionist?			
Do you like to learn and to be intellectually stimulated?			
Do you like to set goals for yourself?			
Do you like to organize and plan?			
Do you easily get frustrated and impatient with people who do not have ambitions or motivation?			
Do your principles and standards cause you to become tired or bored in other people's company?			
Do you like the planning and the challenges of new ideas more than the actual work?			
Do you enjoy delegating and giving responsibilities to others?			

The Test

	Yes	Sometimes	No
Do you have a strong urge to help save our planet?			
If you had enough money would you spend your time travelling around the world for humanistic causes, and would you work actively for peace on earth?			
Are you preoccupied with the universe and everything that has to do with cosmic teachings and development?			
Do you easily see the future in front of you?			
Do you easily get yourself involved in too many projects?			
Do you enjoy entertaining or do you ever have the wish to entertain people?			
Do you feel that you have something to contribute to humanity and do you want to express this to others?			
Is freedom and independence important to you?			
Is your inner belief in God your inspiration and your guide?			
In your work will you follow your beliefs and faith even if it will make other people unhappy?			

	Yes	Sometimes	No
Do you feel that you are more creatively and spiritually developed than most people?			
Do you have a tendency to challenge old dogmatic norms and do you enjoy thinking and developing in new ways?			
Do you easily get involved in leadership positions or become the centre of attention?			
Do you easily get self-occupied and self-centred, because everything you do is about yourself?			
Do you enjoy being your own boss?			
Do you have a lot of ideas and is your source of ideas endless?			
Do you like to hold or would you like to hold workshops, seminars, and courses?			
You do not use money to increase your material situation, but you like to have money in order to do whatever you want to.			
Are you full of passion in sex, and in a monogamous relationship is it easy for you to become unfaithful?			